Western Birds

BACKYARD GUIDE

BILL THOMPSON III

D0048636

COOL
SPRINGS
PRESS
Home and Garden Experts™

MINNEAPOLIS, MINNESOTA

First published in 2013 by Cool Springs Press, an imprint of the Quayside Publishing Group, 400 First Avenue North, Suite 400, Minneapolis, MN 55401

Cool Springs Press titles are also available at discounts in bulk quantity for industrial or sales-promotional use. For details write to Special Sales Manager at Cool Springs Press, 400 First Avenue North, Suite 400, Minneapolis, MN 55401 USA. To find out more about our books, visit us online at www.coolspringspress.com.

ISBN 978-1-59186-555-1

Acquisitions Editor: Billie Brownell
Design Manager: Brad Springer
Cover Design: Michelle Thompson
Interior Design: Mary Rohl
Layout: Danielle Smith

Printed in China
10 9 8 7 6 5 4 3 2 1

Photo Credits
Cover image: Robert McCaw
Jim Burns: pp. 9, 46, 50, 56, 58, 74, 98, 134
Kyle Carlsen: pp. 12, 13, 20 (both), 23
Robert McCaw: pp. 24, 40, 62, 70, 80, 102,
Shutterstock: pp. 8
Brian Small: pp. 6, 42, 48, 52, 54, 60, 64, 66, 68, 72, 82, 84, 86, 88, 90, 92, 94, 96, 104, 106, 108, 110, 112, 114, 116, 118, 120, 122, 124, 126, 128, 132, 136, 138, 140, 142, 144, 146,148
Hugh P. Smith, Jr.: pp. 18
Bill Thompson III: pp. 11, 14, 15, 21 (both), 25, 26, 27, 28 (both), 29, 30 (both), 31, 32, 38, 44, 78, 100,
Michael Williams: pp. 130
Julie Zickefoose: pp. 76

Dedication & Acknowledgments

DEDICATION

To my parents Bill & Elsa Thompson, for having the foresight to start *Bird Watcher's Digest* long before bird watching was a socially acceptable activity. And to all the many subscribers, writers, and other contributors to *BWD* over the years, thanks to you, every day I learn something new and wonderful about birds. And to the birds . . . where would we be without the beauty and wonder of birds?

ACKNOWLEDGMENTS

If you think that creating a book like this is difficult, let me tell you that you're 100 percent correct in that assumption. However, I am fortunate in having so many talented people around me, which makes the book-making process a whole lot easier.

My team at *Bird Watcher's Digest* is without peer in their ability to bring our collective ideas (or my crazy ones) to fruition, whether in print, digital, video, or any other form. Like any major-league team, our roster changes a bit from time to time, but these are the all-stars that I get to write into each day's line-up: Elsa Thompson, Andy Thompson, Ann Kerenyi, Laura Fulton, Katherine Koch, Claire Mullen, Jim Cirigliano, Michelle Barber, Kyle Carlsen, and Wendy Clark. All of these folks helped a great deal in creating this book and I thank them from the bottom of my birdy heart.

Special mention goes to Kyle Carlsen. Kyle is the assistant editor of *Bird Watcher's Digest* and a freelance writer. He received his first pair of binoculars as a gift on his seventh birthday and has been watching birds ever since. He also is the founder of Back Road Birding Tours in southeastern Ohio. Kyle was basically a co-author for this book, writing a large number of species profiles and all the material on the regional birding hotspots. There's no way I would have gotten all of this done without Kyle's help.

Finally, thank you for reading this book (or at least reading *this far* in this book). Authors cannot be authors without people to read what they've written. I hope you find the content we've created to be both useful and interesting. And more than that I hope it helps you to enjoy your backyard birds a lot more in the seasons to come. Happy backyard birding!

Bill Thompson III
Marietta, Ohio   April 2013

CONTENTS

Welcome to Bird Watching in the West

Watching birds, bird watching, or birding—whatever you call it—is one of America's fastest-growing and most popular hobbies. According to a recent survey by the U.S. Fish & Wildlife Service, there are as many as *46 million* bird watchers in the United States. Back in 1978, when my family began publishing *Bird Watcher's Digest* in our living room, bird watching was still considered a bit odd. The image many people associated with bird watching was the character of Miss Jane Hathaway of the television show *The Beverly Hillbillies*. Fortunately, that stereotype is long gone now, and our culture has come to embrace bird watching as an enriching, exciting pursuit—one that can be done with little expense and enjoyed almost anywhere at any time.

WHAT *IS* BIRD WATCHING?

The dictionary defines bird watching as "the identification and observation of wild birds in their natural habitat as a recreation." But as any bird enthusiast can testify, bird watching is a lot more than mere identification and observation. It's about discovery and adventure. It's about attracting and pursuing. It's about connecting with the natural world. And it can be done right in your own backyard.

Sometimes it's hard to know who's doing the watching!

WHY DO WE WANT TO WATCH BIRDS?

Birds have inspired humans for thousands of years. Birds can fly—something we humans have mastered only in the past 100 years. Birds have brilliant plumage, and some even change their colors seasonally. Birds are master musicians, singing beautiful and complex songs. They possess impressive physical abilities—hovering, flying at high speeds, and withstanding extreme weather conditions as well as the rigors of long migration flights. Birds also have behaviors to which we can relate, such as intense courtship displays, devotion to their mates, and the enormous investment of effort spent in raising their young. Sound familiar? In short, birds are a vivid expression of life, and we admire them because they inspire us. This makes us want to know them better and to bring them closer to us. We accomplish this by attracting them to our backyards and gardens, and by using binoculars and other optics to see them more clearly in an "up-close and personal" way.

A house wren fills a backyard with its rich, burbling song.

A BRIEF HISTORY OF BIRD WATCHING

Before the arrival of modern optics that help us view birds more closely, humans used a shotgun approach to bird watching. Literally. Famed ornithologist and bird artist John James Audubon was the first European to document many of the North American bird species in the early 1800s. He did so by shooting every unfamiliar bird he encountered. Having a bird in the hand allowed him to study it closely, and to draw it accurately. This was an excellent method of learning a lot about birds quickly, but it was rather hard on the birds. This method of bird study continued largely unchecked until the early 1900s, when the effects of market hunting on birds became unhappily apparent. In 1934, a young bird enthusiast and artist named Roger Tory Peterson published *A Field Guide to the Birds*, with a system of arrows showing key field marks on the plumage of each species. This enabled a person to identify a bird from a distance, with or without the aid of magnifying optics. Modern bird watching was born, and it was no longer necessary to shoot birds in order to positively identify them. The era of shotgun ornithology was over.

BIRD WATCHING TODAY

Bird watching today is about seeing or hearing birds, attracting them when possible, and then using certain clues to positively identify them. To reach this identification, we use two important tools of the bird-watching trade: binoculars and an identification book. The binoculars (or perhaps a spotting scope, which is a telescope specially designed for nature watching) help you to get a closer, clearer look at the bird. The field guide or other identification book helps you interpret what you see so that you can identify the bird species.

We live in the golden era of bird watching. When I started birding more than 40 years ago, feeders, seed, birdhouses, and other supplies were hard to come by—we had to make our own. Now they are available in almost any store. We can buy a field guide or a book like the one you're holding in any bookstore. We can try out optics at camera stores, outdoor suppliers, bird supply stores, and even at birding festivals (for those who really get into bird watching). We can learn about birds in special bird courses, on the Internet, in magazines, or from DVDs and videos. We can join a local or state bird club and meet new bird-watching friends. We can even take birding tours to far-off places. There's never been a better time to become a bird watcher. So let's get started!

HOW TO GET STARTED:
BASIC GEAR, EQUIPMENT, AND TECHNIQUES

If you're just starting out watching birds, you may need to acquire two basic tools—binoculars and an identification guide—and you've got the second one already!

Binoculars and Other Optics

You may be able to borrow optics from a friend or family member, but as your interest takes off, you'll certainly want to have your own binoculars to use anytime you wish. Fortunately, a decent pair of binoculars can be purchased for less than $100, and some really nice binoculars can be found used on the Internet or through a local bird club for just a bit more. Check out the tip at right for magnification requirements.

Try to find binoculars that are easy and comfortable to use. Make sure they focus easily, giving you a clear image, and that they are comfortable to hold (not too large or heavy) and fit your eye spacing. Every set of eyes is different, so don't settle for binoculars that just don't feel right. The perfect pair of binoculars for you should feel like a natural extension of your hands and eyes. Over time you will become adept at using your optics and, with a little practice, you'll be operating them like a pro.

> ## SEEING CLEARLY
>
> Magnification powers commonly used for bird watching are 7x, 8x, and 10x. This is always the first number listed in the binoculars' description, as in 8 x 40. The second number refers to the size of the objective lens (the big end) of the binocular. The bigger the second number, the brighter the view presented to your eye. In general, for bird-watching binoculars the first number should be between 7x and 10x, and the second number should be between 30 and 45.

Select binoculars that feel good in your hands and are easy to use.

A field guide is one of birding's most essential tools.

Identification Guides

When choosing a field or identification guide, you'll need to decide what type of birding you'll be doing and where you plan to do it. If nearly all of your bird watching will be done at home, then this book is a great introduction! Or, you might want to get a more advanced field guide to the backyard birds of your region, or at least a field guide that limits its scope to your half of the continent. Many field guides are offered in eastern (east of the Rocky Mountains) and western (from the Rockies west) versions. This book, of course, is just for the your part of the country and is naturally more specific to your region. But geographically limited formats include only those birds that are commonly found in that part of the continent, rather than continent-wide guides that include more than 800 North American bird species. If you decide to get a field guide too, choose one that is appropriate for you, and you'll save a lot of searching time—time that can be better spent looking at birds!

Getting to Know the Birds in Your Backyard

Most people who watch birds start out at home, and this usually means getting to know the birds in your backyard. A great way to enhance the diversity of birds in your yard is to set up a simple feeding station. Even a single feeder with the proper food can bring half a dozen or more unfamiliar bird species into your yard. And it's these encounters with new and interesting birds that make watching birds so enjoyable.

Start your feeding station with a feeder geared to the birds that are already in your backyard or garden. For most of us this will mean a tube or hopper feeder filled with sunflower seeds. Place the feeder in a location that offers you a clear view of bird activity, but also offers the birds some nearby cover in the form of a hedge, shrubs, or brush pile into which the birds can fly when a predator approaches. I always set our feeding stations up opposite our kitchen or living room windows because these are the rooms in which we spend most of our daylight hours, and because these rooms have the best windows for bird watching. We'll discuss bird feeding and attracting in greater detail in the next section.

Once you've got a basic feeder set up outside, you'll need to get yourself set up inside your house. You've probably already selected the best location for viewing your feeder. Next you should select a safe place to store your bin-oculars and field guide—somewhere that is easily accessible to you when you suddenly spot a new bird in your backyard. At our house we keep bin-oculars hanging on pegs right next to our kitchen windows. This keeps them handy for use in checking the feeders or for heading out for a walk around our farm.

Hanging a suet feeder is a good way to attract woodpeckers.

BEYOND THE BACKYARD

Sooner or later you may want to expand your bird-watching horizons beyond your backyard bird feeders and bird houses. Birding afield—away from your own home—can be a wonderfully exhilarating experience. Many beginning bird watchers are shy about venturing forth, afraid that their inexperience will prove embarrassing, but there's really no reason to feel this way. The best way to begin birding away from the backyard is to connect with other local bird watchers via your local bird club. Most parts of North America have local or regional bird clubs, and most of these clubs offer regular field trips. Bird watchers are among the friendliest people on the planet, and every bird club is happy to welcome new prospective members. If you don't know how to find a local bird club, ask your friends and neighbors if they know any bird watchers, check the telephone directory, search the Internet, or ask at your area parks, nature centers, and wild bird stores.

Getting out in the field with more experienced bird watchers is the fastest way to improve your skills. Don't be afraid to ask questions ("How did you know that was an indigo bunting?"). Don't worry if you begin to feel overwhelmed by the volume of new information—all new bird watchers experience this. When it happens, relax and take some time to simply watch. In time you'll be identifying birds and looking forward to new challenges and new birds.

Away from feeders, evening grosbeaks eat a variety of seeds, tree buds, and berries.

A daily bird notes diary.

KEEPING A LIST

Many people who become more interested in bird watching enjoy keeping a list of their sightings. This can take the form of a simple written list, notations inside your field guide next to each species' description, or notes in a special journal meant just for such a purpose. There are even software programs available to help you keep your list on your computer. In birding, the most common list is the *life list*. A life list is a list of all the birds you've seen at least once in your life. Let's say you noticed a bright black-and-orange bird in your backyard willow tree one morning, then keyed it out in your field guide to be a male Baltimore oriole. This is a species you'd never seen before, and now you can put it on your life list. List-keeping can be done at any level of involvement, so keep the list or lists that you enjoy. I like to keep a property list of all the species we've seen at least once on our 80-acre farm. Currently, that list is at 186 species, but I'm always watching for something new to show up. I also update my North American life list a couple of times a year, after I've seen a new bird species.

TEN TIPS FOR BEGINNING BIRD WATCHERS

1. Get a decent pair of binoculars, ones that are easy for you to use and hold steady.

2. Find a more advanced field guide to the birds of your region (many guides are divided into eastern and western editions). Guides that cover all the birds of North America contain many birds species uncommon to or entirely absent from your area. You can always upgrade to a continent-wide guide later.

3. Set up a basic feeding station in your yard or garden.

4. Start with your backyard birds. They are the easiest to see, and you can become familiar with them fairly quickly.

5. Practice your identification skills. Starting with a common bird species, note the most obvious visual features of the bird (color, size, shape, and patterns in the plumage). These features are known as field marks and will be helpful clues to the bird's identity.

6. Notice the bird's behavior. Many birds can be identified by their behavior—woodpeckers peck on wood, kingfishers dive for small fish, and swallows are known for their graceful flight.

7. Listen to the bird's sounds. Bird song is a vital component of birding. Learning bird songs and sounds takes a bit of practice, but many birds make it pretty easy for us. For example, chickadees and whip-poor-wills (among others) call out their names. The Resources section of this book contains a listing of tools to help you to learn bird songs.

8. Look at the bird, not at the book. When you see an unfamiliar bird, avoid the temptation to put down your binoculars and begin searching for the bird in your field guide. Instead, watch the bird carefully for as long as it is present—or until you feel certain that you have noted its most important field marks. Then look at your field guide. Birds have wings, and they tend to use them. Your field guide will still be with you long after the bird has gone, so take advantage of every moment to watch an unfamiliar bird while it is present.

9. Take notes. No one can be expected to remember every field mark and description of a bird. But you can help your memory and accelerate your learning by taking notes on the birds you see. These notes can be written in a small pocket notebook, in the margins of your field guide, or even in the back of this book.

10. Venture beyond the backyard and find other bird watchers in your area. The bird watching you'll experience beyond your backyard will be enriching, especially if it leads not only to new birds, but also to new birding friends. Ask a local nature center or wildlife refuge about bird clubs in your region. Your state ornithological organization or natural resources division may also be helpful. Bird watching with other birders can be the most enjoyable of all.

A QUICK GUIDE TO GETTING STARTED

Welcome to the wonderful world of bird watching! To get you started, let me explain how to use this book. The featured birds are in order *taxonomically*—that is, how you'd find them in a bird identification book. That's so we can group birds that are in the same family together—the robin and wood thrush, for example. It will help your identification process to have similar birds closer together so you can flip from one page to another to double-check the photograph.

Each featured bird includes a large photograph, usually a male in breeding plumage, as its identification shot. Bear in mind that female birds and juveniles often have drabber coloring. I've described those in each profile. The topics that most bird watchers want to know are covered:

- **How do I identify it?** This is a physical description of each bird and ways to distinguish it from other similar-looking birds.

- **Where do I find it?** This section describes the bird's preferred habitat, where you are most likely to spot it.

- **What can I feed or do to attract it?** We all want to attract birds to our backyard (well, most birds). This paragraph explains how to create the environment that the bird loves! It includes information on feeders and bird food, as well as creating a habitat with water and plants.

- **Nesting** explains where and how the featured bird builds its nest, including whether it will nest in a birdhouse.

The "At A Glance" chart quickly identifies attributes of the featured bird that will either help you identify it or attract it. An "✔" in the column indicates that the feature applies to the bird in question.

Now—let's get going!
Bill Thompson III

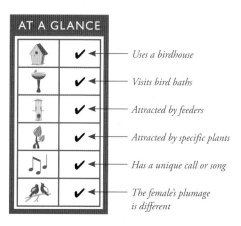

AT A GLANCE

🏠	✔	*Uses a birdhouse*
	✔	*Visits bird baths*
	✔	*Attracted by feeders*
	✔	*Attracted by specific plants*
♪♩	✔	*Has a unique call or song*
	✔	*The female's plumage is different*

Creating a Habitat
Attracting Birds to Your Backyard with Food, Water, Shelter, and Plants

Birds need four basic things to live: food, water for drinking and bathing, a safe place to roost, and a safe place to nest. Believe it or not, these four elements are actually quite easy for you to offer to birds, even if your backyard is small. A bird-friendly backyard has a good feeding station with several feeders and food types; a shallow birdbath with moving water; a variety of shrubs, trees, and other plants for adequate cover and natural nesting opportunities; and a birdhouse or two for cavity-nesting birds, such as chickadees and bluebirds. This chapter will provide you with the tools you need to transform your backyard—no matter the size—into an inviting place for birds throughout the year.

FEEDING BIRDS

Bird feeding is a good place to start your bird-attracting efforts. It's wise to begin with a single feeder, such as a hopper or tube feeder filled with black-oil sunflower seeds. The black-oil sunflower seed is the most common type of sunflower seed available because it's the seed type that most of our feeder birds can readily eat. Think of it as the hamburger of the bird world! The black-oil sunflower seed has a thin shell (easy for seed-eating birds to crack) and a large, meaty seed kernel inside. As you can see from the seed preference chart on page 22, many backyard birds eat sunflower seeds.

A single feeder with the proper food can bring half a dozen bird species to your yard.

Other excellent foods for birds include mixed seed (a blend that normally includes millet, milo, cracked corn, and other seeds), sunflower bits (shells removed), peanuts (best offered unsalted and without the shell), suet or suet cakes, cracked corn, thistle seed (also known as niger or nyjer seed), safflower seed, nectar (for hummingbirds), mealworms, fruits, and berries. Bird feeding varies from region to region—don't be afraid to experiment with new feeders or food. Birds will vote with their bills and stomachs and will let you know their preferences.

Eating the food at feeders is not the only way birds find sustenance. A backyard or garden that includes natural food sources for birds—such as seed-producing flowering plants and fruit-bearing trees and shrubs—will further enhance its attractiveness to birds. In fact, it's often the natural features of a backyard habitat that attract the birds' attention rather than the bird feeders.

Pictured from the top down: Black-oil sunflower seed, peanuts, mixed seed, and safflower seed.

A mourning dove at a platform feeder.

FEEDER TYPES

It's important to match the foods and feeders to each other as well as to the birds you wish to attract. Sunflower seed works in a wide variety of feeders, including tube, hopper, platform, and satellite or excluder feeders (which permit small birds to feed, but exclude larger birds), as well as for ground feeding. Mixed seed does not work as well in tube or hopper feeders for a couple of reasons. First of all, the birds that prefer mixed seed tend to be ground feeders, so it's less natural for them to go to an elevated feeder for food. Secondly, elevated feeder designs (such as tubes or hoppers) are built to dole out seed as it is eaten and the smaller size of most mixed seed kernels causes excess spillage. Mixed seed works best when offered on a platform feeder or when scattered on the ground.

A white-breasted nuthatch at a peanut feeder.

When purchasing your feeders and foods, make sure they will work effectively with one another. Specialty foods such as suet, peanuts, thistle (niger or nyjer), mealworms, fruit, and nectar require specific feeders for the best results for you and the birds. The Food and Feeder Chart on the next page is a great place to start.

FOOD AND FEEDER CHART

SPECIES	FOOD
Quail, Pheasants	Cracked corn, millet, wheat, milo
Pigeons, Doves	Millet, cracked corn, wheat, milo, niger (thistle seed), buckwheat, sunflower, baked goods
Hummingbirds	Plant nectar, small insects, sugar solution
Woodpeckers	Suet, meat scraps, sunflower hearts and seed, cracked corn, peanuts, fruits, sugar solution, mealworms
Jays	Peanuts, sunflower, suet, meat scraps, cracked corn, baked goods
Crows	Meat scraps, suet, cracked corn, peanuts, baked goods, leftovers, dog food
Titmice, Chickadees	Peanut kernels, sunflower, suet, peanut butter, mealworms
Nuthatches	Suet, suet mixes, sunflower hearts and seed, peanut kernels, peanut butter, mealworms
Wrens, Creepers	Suet, suet mixes, peanut butter, peanut kernels, bread, fruit, millet (wrens), mealworms
Mockingbirds, Thrashers, Catbirds	Halved apples, chopped fruit, mealworms, suet nutmeats, millet (thrashers), soaked raisins, currants, sunflower hearts
Robins, Bluebirds, Other Thrushes	Suet, suet mixes, mealworms, berries, baked goods, chopped fruit, soaked raisins, currants, nutmeats, sunflower hearts
Kinglets	Suet, suet mixes, baked goods, mealworms
Waxwings	Berries, chopped fruit, canned peas, currants, dry raisins
Warblers	Suet, suet mixes, fruit, baked goods, sugar solution, chopped nutmeats
Tanagers	Suet, fruit, sugar solution, mealworms, baked goods
Cardinals, Grosbeaks	Sunflower, safflower, cracked corn, millet, fruit
Towhees, Juncos	Millet, sunflower, cracked corn, peanuts, baked goods, nutmeats, mealworms
Sparrows, Buntings	Millet, sunflower hearts, black-oil sunflower, cracked corn, baked goods
Blackbirds, Starlings	Cracked corn, milo, wheat, table scraps, baked goods, suet
Orioles	Halved oranges, apples, berries, sugar solution, grape jelly, suet mixes, soaked raisins, dry mealworms, currants
Finches, Siskins	Thistle (niger), sunflower hearts, black-oil sunflower seed, millet, canary seed, fruit, peanut kernels, suet mixes

SETTING UP
A FEEDING STATION

Place your feeding station in a spot that is useful and attractive to you and the birds. When we moved into our farmhouse, we looked out all the windows before choosing a spot for our feeding station. You may want to do the same thing. After all, the whole point of bird feeding is to be able to see and enjoy the birds. From the birds' perspective, your feeders should be placed adjacent to cover—a place they can leave from and retreat to safely and quickly if a predator appears. This cover can be a woodland edge, brushy area or brush pile, hedges or shrubs, or even a weedy fencerow. If your yard is mostly lawn, consider creating a small island of cover near your feeding station. This will greatly enhance the feeders' appeal to birds.

Be patient. You've spent the money and effort to put up feeders, but don't expect immediate dividends. Birds are creatures of habit, and it may take a few days or even a few weeks before they recognize your offering as a source of food. Sooner or later, a curious chickadee, finch, or sparrow will key into the food source, and the word will spread along the local bird "grapevine."

A tube feeder filled with black-oil sunflower seed is a great way to start your feeding station.

BIRDHOUSES

Almost every bird species builds or uses some type of nest to produce and rear its young. However, only a small fraction of our backyard birds use nest boxes provided by humans. Birds that use nest boxes or birdhouses are called "cavity nesters" because they prefer to nest inside an enclosed space, such as hole excavated in a tree, as many woodpeckers do. Nest boxes simulate a natural cavity, but they have the added advantage (for humans) of our being able to place them in a convenient spot. To the birds' advantage, we can protect the nest box from predators, bad weather, and other problems.

Being a landlord to the birds is a thrilling experience. You are treated to an intimate peek inside the lives of your "tenants" and rewarded with the presence of their offspring, if nesting is successful. To help ensure the nesting success of your birds you need to provide the proper housing in an appropriate setting, and you should monitor the housing during the nesting season.

Gambel's quail occasionally visit backyards in the southwestern states for mixed seed and cracked corn.

The Right Housing

Two factors are key to providing the right nest box for your birds: the size of the housing and the size of the entry hole. Not all cavity nesters are picky about the interior dimensions of the cavity, except when it is excessively big or small. But the size of the entry hole is important because it can effectively limit the entrance of large, aggressive nest competitors, predators, and inclement weather. For example, an entry hole with a diameter of 1½ inches on a bluebird nest box will permit entry by bluebirds and many smaller birds, including chickadees, titmice, nuthatches, wrens, and tree swallows. But this same size keeps European starlings out and prevents them from usurping the box.

An Appropriate Setting

Place your nest boxes where they will be most likely to be found and used by birds. Bluebirds and swallows prefer nest sites in the middle of large, open, grassy areas. Wrens, chickadees, nuthatches, flycatchers, woodpeckers, and other woodland birds prefer sites that are in or adjacent to woodlands. Robins, phoebes, Carolina wrens, barn swallows, and purple martins prefer to nest near human dwellings, perhaps for the protection from predators that we provide.

Monitoring Your Nest Boxes

By taking a weekly peek inside your nest boxes, you will stay abreast of your tenants' activities, and you'll be able to help them raise their families successfully. During most of the year, your birdhouses will appear to be empty. This does not mean that the boxes are going unused. In fact, many birds use nest boxes during the winter months as nighttime roosts. A loose feather, insect parts, berry seeds, or a few droppings are classic evidence of roosting activity.

Bluebird eggs.

During breeding season, your regular visits will help you know when nest building begins and when eggs are laid, and will give you an idea about how soon the eggs will hatch and the babies leave the nest. Bird nests are vulnerable to a variety of dangers, including harsh weather and predators such as cats, raccoons, snakes, and even other birds, as well as nest-site competitors. These dangers are greatly reduced when nest boxes are monitored because the birds' landlord (you) can take steps to protect the nest.

On my trips to check each of our ten nest boxes, I keep a small notebook with me to record my observations. Each nest box has its own name and number in my notebook, along with the date of each visit and a note about what I've found.

Chickadee nestlings.

When nesting starts in a box I note the date, what materials are used to construct the nest, and the date that the first egg was laid. Once the clutch is complete and the female begins incubating the eggs, I can estimate the hatching date. This usually takes about 14 days. Another 14 to 21 days later, I know the young birds will be ready to leave the nest.

Peeking Inside

When checking a nest box, approach quietly. During the breeding season, you may scare the female off the nest temporarily when you open the box. Don't worry. If you keep your visit brief, she'll be back to the nest soon. I visit nest boxes in the late morning on sunny days, when the adult birds are likely to be away finding food. I open the box, quickly count the eggs or young, close the box and move away before pausing to record my notes. It's a myth that opening a nest box or checking the young will cause the adults to abandon the nest. In fact, over time many cavity-nesting birds that use nest boxes grow quite accustomed to regular visits.

One final note on nest monitoring. As fledging time approaches for the young birds—normally about two weeks after the eggs hatch—you should curtail your box visits to avoid causing a premature nest departure.

When Things Go Wrong

You open your nest box, and you find broken or missing eggs and the nest in disarray. What happened? The bad news is: a predator has raided your nest, and, in the natural order of things, the eggs or nestlings have been eaten. The good news is: there are steps that you can take to avoid such an event in the future.

It's important to protect your nest boxes so predators cannot easily access them. For many homeowners, the best option is to mount the housing on galvanized metal poles with pole-mounted predator baffles installed beneath the boxes. An added advantage to pole-mounting (as opposed to mounting on a fencepost or tree) is that the housing can be moved to a new location fairly easily.

You may wish to consult one of the publications listed in the Resources section for specific strategies for dealing with nest box predators and pests.

An example of a pole-mounted predator baffle. The slick metal surface discourages climbing.

CREATING A BACKYARD BIRD HABITAT

To make your backyard or garden a haven for birds, all you need to do is think like a bird. Look around your yard. Where is the food, the water? Where are the places to hide from predators or to shelter in bad weather? Is nesting habitat available?

Black-eyed Susans provide food for birds.

An ideal bird habitat can be created in a tiny urban garden just as it can be created in a large rural setting. Birds love varied habitats, so when you are planning your yard, landscape, or gardens, resist the urge to plant matching plants in straight lines. Instead, let your imagination go wild—literally. Give the edges of beds or gardens natural curves. Scatter trees, shrubs, and vines in clumps or islands around the area you are designing. On the edges of your property, try to create natural transitions from the grass of your yard to the tops of your trees with short and medium-height plants that provide food and shelter for birds.

Edible Habitat

Birds have evolved over millions of years right alongside the native plants with which they share the planet. These same native plants can work for you in your bird-friendly habitat plan. Your local nursery, nature center, or native plant society should be able to recommend plant species that are native to your region. Native plants not only provide food in the form of fruits and nuts, but birds may also eat the plants' buds, leaves, nectar, and sap, as well as the insects that live on the plants. When choosing your native plants, select a wide variety of species, sizes, shapes, and seasonality. Planting only one or two plant species will minimize the number of birds your habitat will attract.

Black raspberry plants provide a natural food source for backyard birds.

Water

Birds need water all year long for drinking and bathing. The best way to offer water to birds is in a shallow birdbath with about 2 inches of water in it. I've always had good luck attracting birds to water in my yard when the bath was on or near the ground and when the water had some motion to it.

The sight and sound of moving water are highly attractive to birds. You can add motion to any birdbath or water feature with a mister, dripper, or a recirculating pump. Misters and drippers attach to your garden hose and release a small amount of water that disturbs the surface of the bath; these ripples are eye-catchingly attractive to birds. Recirculating pumps, which require electricity, recycle the water from the main bath through a pump and filter and then back to the bath. If you live in an area where water freezes in winter, add a small electric birdbath heater to keep the water open and available to birds.

If you already have a water garden or water feature, consider making part of it accessible to birds. This can be accomplished by placing a flat rock shelf on or near the water's surface, or by allowing recirculating water to trickle over an exposed flat rock. Our backyard water garden is ringed with goldfinches almost every day all year round. They use a large, flat piece of slate that gets splashed by our small waterfall as a place to grab a quick drink.

Water is a universal attractant for birds—species that might otherwise never visit your yard, feeders, or birdhouses will visit a clean and alluring birdbath or water feature.

Moving water is irresistible to birds.

A male house finch rests in a raspberry tangle.

Shelter

When they need to rest, hide from danger, or get out of the weather, birds seek deep cover in the form of thick vegetation, vine tangles, dense evergreens, or brushy areas. These bits of habitat may not be first on a landscaper's list of backyard beautifying accents, but to a bird they are vital havens. Even a brush pile in a corner of your property can offer enough shelter during a storm to help sparrows, cardinals, and other backyard birds survive.

Look at your bird habitat, and observe where the birds go just before a storm or at dusk. These are the places in which they shelter themselves. Consider adding more habitat, and your yard will be even more attractive to birds.

A variety of plant types helps attract more backyard birds.

The more your backyard looks like nature, the more attractive it will be for birds.

Places to Nest

The majority of North American birds do not use nest boxes. Most build their nests in places that are hidden from view—in trees, bushes, or secluded spots on or near the ground. Some birds—such as phoebes, barn swallows, and Carolina wrens—are bold enough to build nests on porch ledges, in garages, and in barns. House finches and mourning doves are known for building their nests in hanging flower baskets, but these sites won't satisfy most of our birds.

The places where birds choose to nest are similar to the places they choose to roost and shelter—in thick vegetation and deep cover out of view of passing predators. In providing a nesting habitat for birds, the key is diversity. As you read through the species profiles in this book, notice the habitat features that each species prefers. Then factor this information into your habitat plans.

Helping Other Nesting Birds

There are many things you can do to help non–cavity nesters—all those birds that build open-cup nests and will never use one of our nest boxes. The most important thing is to offer variety in your landscaping or backyard habitat. A backyard that is mostly lawn with a tree or two staked out in the middle will not be nearly as appealing as a yard featuring a variety of plant types, including grasses, perennial plants, shrubs, bushes, trees, and other natural elements. The more your landscape looks like nature, the more attractive it will be for birds.

BIRD-FRIENDLY LANDSCAPING TIPS
FOR WESTERN GARDENS

The West includes so many different eco-regions and habitats that it's almost impossible to make just one set of simple recommendations. From the south-western deserts to the rainy Pacific Northwest, and the high mountain meadows

An example of a bird-friendly backyard: weedy edges, a nice variety of trees, flowering plants for hummingbirds, shaded areas, and well-situated viewing spots for year-round enjoyment.

of the Rockies to the lush Pacific Coast of California, the West has a vast array of habitats and the bird variety to go with it. Here are some tips and plant suggestions for making your western backyard as bird-friendly as possible:

- Seek expert local advice for your specific growing zone and local eco-region. This will help you choose native plants and noninvasive exotics that are good for birds and adapted to your local conditions.

- Don't forget the water. In many areas of the West it's a source of water that makes the difference between a basic landscape and one that is friendly to birds and wildlife. Numerous western birds will visit a reliable source of water. It doesn't have to be fancy.

- The West is home to more hummingbird species than anywhere else in North America. Include nectar-producing plants in your landscape plan to ensure that you can enjoy these tiny, sparkling beauties throughout the year.

- Great hummingbird plants include hummingbird mint, California fuchsia, cardinal flower, royal penstemon, desert beardtongue, chuparosa, ocotillo, desert willow, western red columbine, orange honeysuckle, and New Mexico locust.

- Cover for ground-feeding birds is important in the West, where several quail, sparrow, and thrasher species are regular visitors to backyard feeders. These birds need cover nearby to escape into when the neighborhood Cooper's hawk swoops in for its dinner.

- Add these flowering plants, grasses, and vines for birds: agapanthus, crocosmias, columbines, calendula, purple coneflowers, scarlet creepers, golden yarrow, lupines, poppies, and salvias.

PLACES FOR YOU

As you plan for your bird-friendly habitat, you'll also want to incorporate elements that you can use and enjoy, such as bird-attracting plants, a water garden, benches, shady relaxation spots, and perhaps a location for your feeding station. Remember, the whole point of attracting birds to your property is so that you can enjoy them while they enjoy your offerings. Plan with your favorite viewing spots in mind, and you'll be rewarded with year-round free (and natural) entertainment.

BIRD-FRIENDLY PLANTS FOR YOUR BACKYARD

TREES

Common Name	Latin Name	Good For/Other Notes
Apple	*Malus* spp.	Fruit, insects, nesting cavities
Ash	*Fraxinus* spp.	Seeds, insects, cover
Aspen	*Populus* spp.	Seeds, insects, cover, nesting cavities
Birch	*Betula* spp.	Seeds, insects, cover
Cedar	*Juniperus* spp.	Fruit, year-round cover
Cherry	*Prunus* spp.	Fruit
Chokecherry, Common	*Prunus virginiana*	Fruit
Cottonwood	*Populus* spp.	Nesting cavities, shelter
Crabapple	*Malus* spp.	Fruit, insects
Dogwood	*Cornus* spp.	Fruit
Fir	*Abies* spp.	Year-round cover
Hackberry	*Celtis* spp.	Fruit, cover
Hawthorn	*Crataegus* spp.	Fruit, cover, nesting
Hemlock	*Tsuga* spp.	Seeds, insects, shelter
Holly	*Ilex* spp.	Fruit, year-round cover
Juniper	*Juniperus* spp.	Year-round cover
Larch	*Larix* spp.	Seeds
Madrone	*Arbutus* spp.	Fruit
Maple	*Acer* spp.	Seeds, cover
Mesquite	*Prosopis* spp.	Shelter
Mountain Ash	*Sorbus* spp.	Fruit
Mulberry, Red	*Morus rubra*	Fruit
Oak	*Quercus* spp.	Acorns, cover, insects
Pine	*Pinus* spp.	Year-round cover, insects
Poplar	*Populus* spp.	Nesting cavities, shelter
Sassafras	*Sassafras albidum*	Fruit, cover, nesting cavities
Shadbush (Serviceberry)	*Amelanchier laevis*	Fruit, flowers
Spruce	*Picea* spp.	Year-round cover
Sycamore	*Platanus* spp.	Nesting cavities, shelter, insects
Willow	*Salix* spp.	Nesting cavities, shelter, insects

SHRUBS		
Common Name	*Latin Name*	*Good For/Other Notes*
Arrowwood Viburnum	*Viburnum dentatum*	Fall fruit; tolerates shade
Bayberry, Northern	*Myrica pensylvanica*	Fruit; male & female plants needed for fruit
Blackberry, American	*Rubus allegheniensis*	Fruit; dense cover; nesting
Blueberry, Highbush	*Vaccinium corymbosum*	Fruit, flowers, cover; needs acid soil
Chokeberry, Red	*Aronia arbutifolia*	Fruit; moist soil preferred
Cranberry, Highbush	*Viburnum trilobum*	Fruit; shade tolerant
Dogwood	*Cornus* spp.	Fall fruit; dense cover
Elderberry, American	*Sambucus canadensis*	Fruit; dense cover
Hercules' Club	*Aralia spinosa*	Fruit
Hobblebush	*Viburnum alnifolium*	Fruit; shade tolerant
Holly, Deciduous	*Ilex decidua, Ilex* spp.	Winter fruit; male & female plants needed for fruit
Huckleberry, Black	*Gaylussacia baccata*	Fruit; sandy soil preferred
Inkberry	*Ilex glabra*	Fruit; thicket forming; needs acid soil
Mahonia	*Mahonia aquifolium*	Fruit; year-round cover
Manzanita	*Arctostaphylos* spp.	Early fruit; thick cover
Nannyberry	*Viburnum lentago*	Fruit; shade-tolerant
Pokeweed	*Phytolacca americana*	Fall fruit
Rose	*Rosa* spp.	Winter fruit; summer flowers
Shadbush	*Amelanchier* spp.	Early fruit
Spicebush	*Lindera benzoin*	Fruit; needs moist soil
Sumac	*Rhus* spp.	Fruit available all winter
Viburnum	*Viburnum* spp.	Fall fruit; tolerates shade
Winterberry, Common	*Ilex verticillata*	Fruit; male & female plants needed for fruit
Yew	*Taxus* spp.	Year-round cover; some fruit

(CONTINUED FROM PREVIOUS PAGE)

VINES		
Common Name	*Latin Name*	*Good For/Other Notes*
Ampelopsis, Heartleaf	*Ampelopsis cordata*	Fruit; resembles a grape vine
Bittersweet, American	*Celastrus scandens*	Fruit; avoid Asian species
Grapes, Wild	*Vitis* spp.	Fruit; cover; attracts 100 species
Greenbriars	*Smilax* spp.	Fruit; thick cover
Trumpet Honeysuckle	*Lonicera sempervirens*	Nectar; fruit; cover; avoid Asian species
Trumpet Vine	*Campsis radicans*	Nectar; summer cover
Virginia Creeper	*Parthenocissus quinquefolia*	Fruit; attracts 40 species

FLOWERS		
Common Name	*Latin Name*	*Good For/Other Notes*
Aster	*Aster* spp.	Flowers; seeds; attracts butterflies
Bachelor's Button	*Centaurea cyanus*	Seeds
Black-Eyed Susan	*Rudbeckia serotina*	Seeds
Blazing Star	*Liatris* spp.	Seeds; flowers attract butterflies
California Poppy	*Eschscholzia californica*	Seeds
Coneflower, Purple	*Echinacea purpurea*	Seeds; flowers attract butterflies
Coreopsis	*Coreopsis* spp.	Seeds; flowers attract butterflies
Cornflower	*Centaurea cyanus*	Seeds
Cosmos	*Cosmos* spp.	Seeds
Daisy, Gloriosa	*Rudbeckia* cv.	Seeds
Goldenrod	*Solidago* spp.	Flowers for butterflies; winter cover
Joe-Pye Weed	*Eupaorium* spp.	Flowers for butterflies; winter cover
Marigold	*Tagetes* spp.	Seeds
Penstemon	*Penstemon* spp.	Nectar; seeds
Poppy	*Papaver* spp.	Seeds; flowers attract butterflies

FLOWERS		
Common Name	*Latin Name*	*Good For/Other Notes*
Primrose	*Oenothera* spp.	Seeds
Sedum	*Sedum* spp.	Seeds; flowers attract butterflies
Sunflower	*Helianthus* spp.	Seeds
Thistle, Globe	*Echinops* spp.	Flowers; seeds; nesting material
Zinnia	*Zinnnia elegans*	Seeds; flowers attract butterflies

INTERESTING BIRD FACTS

- A house wren can feed 500 spiders and caterpillars to its nestlings during a single summer afternoon.

- A chimney swift can devour 1,000 flying insects in a single day.

- A barn owl can swallow a large rat whole. After digesting its meal, the owl coughs up a pellet containing the rat's bones and fur.

- A Baltimore oriole can eat as many as 17 hairy caterpillars in a minute.

- Quail, sparrows, and other seed-eating birds sometimes swallow fine gravel, which they store in a special part of their digestive system. This gravel, known as grit, helps to break up hard seeds to make them easier to digest.

- More than 70 different bird species have been observed drinking nectar from hummingbird feeders.

- Starlings love to adorn their nest cavities with shiny or colorful things such as coins, bits of plastic, and other birds' feathers.

- A tundra swan's plumage contains more than 25,000 feathers.

- Herons and egrets were once shot by the thousands so that their ornate feathers could be used to decorate women's hats. The shooting of most migratory birds is now illegal.

- Peregrine falcons may reach speeds of 200 miles per hour when diving for prey. They use their balled-up talons to knock out their prey, then catch the hapless, falling bird before it hits the ground or water.

Profiles of Backyard Birds of the West

In the following pages we've created a handy guide to fifty-five of the most common backyard birds of the West. These include common feeder visitors, year-round resident species, birds that are present during the nesting seasons, and a few others that you're sure to encounter at some point in your yard or nearby. During the course of your bird watching, you'll probably see other birds passing through your yard that are not included here—after all there are *hundreds* of bird species that may be seen in the West each year. At the back of this book there are some pages where you can record your backyard bird sightings and observations. I hope you'll enjoy these species profiles, and have some fun along the way. Happy backyard bird watching!

Sharp-shinned Hawk

If the birds at your feeder seem skittish, they have a good reason—a sharp-shinned hawk could appear at any moment. Its primary prey, after all, is small songbirds. This songbird specialist is actually doing nature a favor by weeding out the slowest, weakest, or oldest birds, helping to keep bird populations healthy. Once thought to be an evil killer of innocent birds, thousands of sharpies and other hawks used to be shot, a practice that has since been outlawed. Your first reaction to a sharp-shinned hawk in your backyard might be horror, but you have to respect the bird's ability as a predator. Watch the

hawk's intense focus when it's perched, and listen for how the songbirds warn each other about the hawk. It's like a television nature show, live from your living room window!

HOW DO I IDENTIFY IT?

Sharp-shinned hawks are built for speed and maneuverability with short rounded wings, a slender body, and long narrow tail. They fly like a jet fighter as they chase fleeing songbirds into and through thick cover. Adult sharpies have reddish breasts and a dark gray head and back. Young birds have brown backs and white breasts coarsely streaked with brown. Sharpies appear small-headed and smaller-bodied when compared to the similar, but larger, Cooper's hawk. Flying sharpies almost always follow this rhythm: flap, flap, flap, glide.

WHERE DO I FIND IT?

Forest habitats of almost any type are home to sharp-shinned hawks, but they are most likely to be found where songbird populations are thriving. Sharpies have a vast breeding range, but they prefer large tracts of woodland for nest sites, so they are rarely observed on the nest. In fall most migrate southward, their movement triggered by passing cold fronts. Some migrate as far as Central America, but many spend the winter in the continental United States.

WHAT CAN I FEED OR DO TO ATTRACT IT?

While many people may not wish to attract a sharp-shinned hawk to their property, if you have small birds at your feeders or in your gardens, sooner or later they will attract the attention of a passing hawk. Hunting sharp-shinned hawks use surprise and speed—emerging suddenly from behind a line of trees or bursting forth from a quiet, concealed perch. As surprised birds scatter, the sharpie pursues one and grabs it with its long, taloned toes. If undisturbed, the hawk may finish its meal on the ground, or it may carry it away to a safer location. Sharpies will take prey as large as ruffed grouse and as small as hummingbirds.

NESTING

The nest of the sharp-shinned hawk is usually well hidden. In fact, you are more likely to hear the adults calling to one another as they share the nesting and feeding duties than actually see them. The nest is made of sticks and is built by the female high in a tree. She lays four to five eggs and incubates them for about a month. After hatching, the female broods the young birds for about 20 days, all the while being fed by her mate. A month after hatching, young hawks are ready to leave the nest, though they spend several more weeks being fed by the parents.

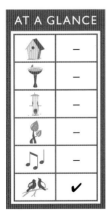

AT A GLANCE	
🏠	—
⛲	—
🔯	—
🌿	—
♫♪	—
🐦🐦	✔

Cooper's Hawk

Cooper's hawks often perch in inconspicuous places, shooting through the branches or dropping from trees to nab unsuspecting prey. A flurry of fearful birds and a gray flash may mark the arrival of a Cooper's hawk to your backyard. Cooper's hawks are medium-sized hawks and formidable hunters that are usually seen singly except during migration.

Cooper's hawks are attracted to what bird feeders attract—birds!— helping to maintain the natural balance between predator and prey, even in the suburbs. When successful, Cooper's hawks usually weed out the birds that are sick, old, or otherwise less than perfectly healthy. They will not scare birds from your feeders for very long. Soon after the hawk departs, the activity at your feeder will return to normal.

HOW DO I IDENTIFY IT? It can be a little confusing to see the difference between the Cooper's hawk and the similar sharp-shinned hawk. Adults of both species have similar markings, as do their brown-backed immatures (birds that are less than a year old). Size is often not a trustworthy identification tool in the field—proportions and tail edges are more telling. Compared with the sharp-shinned hawk, the Cooper's has a proportionately larger head and neck and a rounded (not notched) or square-tipped tail (as does the sharp-shinned). Perched, adult Cooper's hawks often show a color contrast between a dark crown and gray back. In flight, a Cooper's hawk's head sticks out well past the front edge of the wings, and the end of its tail usually looks rounded. Sharp-shinned hawks look like a capital "T" in flight, their shorter heads almost even with the front edge of their wings.

WHERE DO I FIND IT? In many areas, Cooper's hawks are uncommon nesters. Far-northern birds generally winter to the south. You can look for Cooper's hawks in any type of forest, along forest edges, and in woods near watercourses. But don't be surprised if you find one elsewhere, particularly in winter and fall. They seem to be adapting to suburban life, nesting near backyards or in city parks. During spring and fall, migrating Cooper's hawks gravitate toward ridges and coasts.

WHAT CAN I FEED OR DO TO ATTRACT IT? These hawks are not attracted to seed at feeders—they are attracted to the birds at your feeders. Cooper's hawks generally feed on midsized birds, including robins, flickers, doves, and pigeons, but they also eat small mammals, including chipmunks and squirrels. Insects and reptiles are sometimes featured on the menu. If you have a backyard with a bit of woodland and some active feeders, a Cooper's hawk is a likely visitor.

NESTING Cooper's hawks place their bulky stick nests high on horizontal branches in large trees, sometimes building them atop another large bird or squirrel nest. The female lays three to five eggs and incubates them for about five weeks. The male brings food, but the female feeds it to the young, which usually take flight about four or five weeks after hatching. Both adults and young birds can be quite vocal around the nest. The typical call is a loud *kik-kik-kik-kik* that sounds like an angry woodpecker.

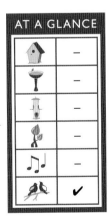

AT A GLANCE	
🏠	–
(bird bath)	–
(feeder)	–
(leaf)	–
♫	–
(birds)	✔

Rock Pigeon

Originating in northern Europe, Africa, and India, rock pigeons—largely gone from their former wild haunts—have spread to cities and towns worldwide thanks to their domestication 5,000 years ago. Evidence of domestication lies in their highly variable coloration; a flock may contain birds in every color, from pure white to reddish to solid black. Rock pigeons are nonmigratory, though pigeon racing clubs worldwide exploit their celebrated homing skills. Older field guides and bird books may refer to this species as rock dove and feral pigeon. Some backyard bird watchers also refer to these birds as sky rats or feeder pigs. Why? Because they can clear out a feeder faster than a vacuum cleaner.

Thanks to pigeons' flocking habit, most homeowners are less than delighted when they visit. The most effective deterrents seem to be sturdy feeders enclosed by wire caging that excludes the larger-bodied pigeons while admitting smaller birds. Some people spread food for rock pigeons far away from the main feeding stations to keep the pigeons from overwhelming seed feeders.

HOW DO I IDENTIFY IT?   A chunky-bodied bird with a small head, deep chest, powerful wings, and a square tail, the rock pigeon is built for flight. Wild-type birds are slate blue with a white rump, black terminal tail band, and two black bars on the inside back edges of the gray wings. In bright sunlight you may see the pinkish green iridescence on the neck. Pigeons have short, reddish legs and a short, straight bill. Their song is a series of soft, resonant coos—*ooh-ga-rooogh*—and a harsh *woogh!* serves as an alarm call. Pigeons are almost always found in flocks except when tending young.

WHERE DO I FIND IT?   It is rare to find rock pigeons in natural habitats, though there are still some cliff-nesting populations in North America along rivers and rocky ocean coasts. Most rock pigeons prefer tall buildings, with their many ledges, to be ideal nesting sites. These same pigeons are happy to take food, such as bread and popcorn, from city sidewalks. In suburban areas they can be found nesting under bridges, and in rural areas, in old barns.

WHAT CAN I FEED OR DO TO ATTRACT IT?   Walking and pecking with rapidly bobbing heads, pigeons find their preferred food—grains, seeds, and some fruits—on the ground. Pigeons will eat anything that might be offered, but millet and cracked corn are special favorites. If you really wish to attract rock pigeons, toss mixed seed on the ground beneath your feeders. Urban birds have highly developed scavenging skills, raiding trashcans and fast food litter for tasty morsels of food.

NESTING   The male's spinning, bowing, and cooing is a common sight on city sidewalks. Pigeons mate for life, with the males guarding females zealously. They may lay eggs and raise young anytime. Building ledges, highway overpasses, barns, bridges, and other structures may be selected as the site on which to build a stick-and-grass nest and lay two eggs. Both males and females incubate for about 18 days. The rubbery, black-skinned squabs stay in the nest 25 to 45 days. Because they are common and accustomed to human activity, the rock pigeon is a very easy bird to see and watch. Many urban schools study rock pigeons as a part of their science classes.

AT A GLANCE

	—
	✔
	✔
	—
	✔
	—

Eurasian Collared-Dove

Some North American bird species are native and are beloved backyard friends. Others are like obnoxious relatives who come from far away and over-stay their welcome. The Eurasian collared-dove is one of these. A medium-sized dove that is native to Asia, the Eurasian collared-dove has spread across much of the globe, usually preferring to live in close proximity to humans. If it weren't for a messy burglary of a pet shop in the Bahamas in the 1970s, we might not have the Eurasian collared-dove as a common (and spreading) nesting bird in the New World. After its release, it began colonizing Florida in the 1980s. Today this bird is found all across the western two-thirds of North America, as far north as Alaska. In some areas its numbers have grown so significantly that it is considered a pest. Look for these doves perched on utility poles, wires, and rooftops, where its chunky, square-tailed shape is easily recognized.

HOW DO I IDENTIFY IT?   The Eurasian collared-dove is larger and chunkier-looking than the familiar mourning dove and about the same size as a rock pigeon. It shares the mourning dove's pale tannish gray coloration, but where a mourning dove's tail is long and tapered, the collared-dove's is squared off at the end. Adults have a uniform black half-collar on the nape of the neck, which gives this species its name. The Eurasian collared-dove is a powerful, direct flyer and, when in flight, it shows obvious white patches in the tail. The bill is black and the legs are reddish. The call is a repetitive (and somewhat owl-like) *who-HOO-huh, who-HOO-huh.*

WHERE DO I FIND IT?   The short answer is: almost everywhere. This dove is a resident throughout its range, meaning that it does not migrate seasonally as do many of our songbirds. It thrives in human-altered habitats. They are at home and equally successful in urban, suburban, and rural settings as long as there is a reliable food source available, such as a bird feeder, croplands, a grain elevator, or a farm feedlot. For most of us, we'll hear this bird before we see it, since it calls regularly all day long, especially during the breeding season. Having said that, the Eurasian collared-dove perches in obvious places, so it's not that hard to see.

WHAT CAN I FEED OR DO TO ATTRACT IT?   Eurasian collared-doves are ground-feeders that eat seeds and grain for much of their diet. Their rapid spread across North America has been abetted by backyard bird feeders, and by spilled grain at silos and in animal feedlots. They need open, grassy spaces for foraging and areas of thick vegetation (medium-sized trees and vine tangles) for nesting. They will also forage in areas where weed seeds are left over after the growing season. Thanks to their adaptive nature, the Eurasian collared-dove takes advantage of almost any bird-friendly habitat you provide. This species will regularly visit a backyard water feature or birdbath.

AT A GLANCE

🏠	–
🛁	✔
🌾	✔
🪵	–
♪♩	✔
🕊🕊	–

NESTING   The male calls to the female from various possible nesting sites on buildings and in trees. After she selects one, he brings her nesting materials (grass, twigs, feathers, rootlets) as she builds it. Two white eggs are laid and incubated for slightly more than two weeks. Young doves fledge about 17 days later and shortly thereafter the parents may begin another nesting cycle.

Mourning Dove

Whether you regard them as songbirds or gamebirds, if you feed birds, you probably have mourning doves as constant companions. These tapered, graceful brown and pinkish birds wholeheartedly embrace human alterations of the natural landscape. In fact, mourning doves are most common in agricultural and suburban areas. Doves love water, but may foul birdbaths by sitting around the rim, tails in, letting their droppings fall into the water. Streamlined, fast, and powerful flyers, mourning doves travel in flocks, descending to feed on a great variety of grains and weed seeds that they peck from the ground.

HOW DO I IDENTIFY IT?   The mourning dove is a slender, long-tailed bird compared to the equally common rock pigeon. They are tannish gray overall with a pointed tail that shows obvious white spots along its tapered edges. The mournful *oooahh, oooh, ooh, ooh* song of the mourning dove is a very familiar backyard sound, echoing from power lines and treetops in early spring. When startled into sudden flight, their wings make a whistling sound.

WHERE DO I FIND IT?   Like the Eurasian collard-dove, the mourning dove is found almost everywhere. The only habitat shunned by mourning doves is deep, contiguous forest. They are most common in agricultural areas with hedgerows and shelterbelts. They are often seen in ranks on power lines over farm fields. They are also abundant in suburban areas, where visits to feeding stations are an integral part of their daily routines. Mourning doves migrate, especially far northern populations, but some individuals are resident year-round.

WHAT CAN I FEED OR DO TO ATTRACT IT?   Mourning doves take any seeds that might be offered at feeders, preferring sunflower seeds, cracked corn, millet, milo, and other grains found in seed mixes. They are experts at emptying feeders and can consumer large amounts in a single visit. Afterwards it is common to see a small flock of mourning doves settle in on a nearby perch to relax while they digest their large meal. Open, grassy or weedy areas are attractive to mourning doves, which prefer to feed on the ground. They prefer to roost in dense cover, such as evergreen trees, and may also use these same trees for nesting.

NESTING   Mourning doves may mate and nest in any month of the year, but males begin to tune up their songs in late winter. They have a production-line breeding mode, following one brood with another as often as six times in a season. The twig nest platform—placed in a wide variety of tree species, but frequently in a pine—is often so flimsy that eggs show through from beneath. Two eggs are incubated by both members of the pair, and they hatch in 14 days. Young doves are fed first on crop milk, a secretion unique to the pigeon family, and later on regurgitated seeds. Young remain in the nest for another 15 days but may fledge much earlier. The male feeds them until about day 30, while the female re-nests. Immature birds are visibly smaller and have fine, buff feather edges overall. Mourning doves travel in flocks for much of the year, breaking away only to find a mate, nest, and raise young. Males defend their mates as a kind of mobile territory, defending her and the immediate nest site—but not much else—from other birds.

AT A GLANCE	
🏠	–
🍸	✔
🪹	✔
🦟	–
🎵	✔
🐦	–

Common Ground-Dove

This very small dove can be overlooked as it walks along the ground, lightly bobbing its head with each step, while foraging for seeds. Its scaly neck and breast and sandy-colored back help it to blend into its surroundings. While small flocks of ground-doves often feed in the open, they never seem to be very far away from grassy or brushy habitat into which they can flee if a predator approaches or danger threatens.

HOW DO I IDENTIFY IT? At just 6½ inches in length, the common ground-dove is the smallest of our commonly encountered dove species—about half the size of the widespread and familiar mourning dove. In fact, it's small enough to be mistaken for a sparrow. When perched or sitting on the ground, its plumage is good camouflage. A sandy-tan back and wings spotted with black, and a paler breast, head, and neck scaled with white, make up this bird's initial appearance. When disturbed or startled, the ground-dove bursts into the air in a loud flutter of wings and heads for deeper cover. In flight the common ground-dove's most identifiable field marks are obvious: large rufous patches in the rounded wings and a stubby black tail. A closer look reveals bright red eyes and a pinkish bill tipped in black. The common ground-dove's call is a rising *woot-woot-woot* repeated on the same note in a series.

WHERE DO I FIND IT? This is a bird of open, brushy areas, farmlands, orchards, pinewoods, savannas, and weedy roadsides across the southeastern United States. In the Southwest it can be found in more arid settings, such as brushy thickets or mesquite scrub, often near a source of water. Look for ground-doves on the ground, walking quietly along, pecking at weed seeds and other food. When not foraging on the ground, they roost in trees, resting while they digest the food they have recently consumed. Ground-doves are quick to take advantage of disturbed, burned, mowed, or logged areas where weeds produce large seed crops.

WHAT CAN I FEED OR DO TO ATTRACT IT? Common ground-doves prefer a combination of open, weedy ground and brushy habitat. If you live within their range—across the southernmost portions of the United States from Florida to California—you can attract them by allowing a part of your property become naturally "messy." You can also attract them by scattering mixed seed, finely cracked corn, millet, milo, and other seeds on the ground within a few yards of thick cover. A low platform feeder works just as well, if you do not like scattering seed on the ground. Like all doves, common ground-doves will regularly patronize a source of clean water like a birdbath or water feature, especially those that are at or near ground level.

NESTING While males and females take part in the nest building, the common ground-dove is not going to win any awards for nest architecture. Their nests are either a shallow depression on the ground lined with a few grasses or a flimsy, flat platform of sticks placed low in a thicket or vine tangle. One to three eggs are laid and incubated by the parents for about two weeks. Hatchlings remain in the nest for 10 to 13 days before fledging. Adults may produce multiple broods in a year.

AT A GLANCE	
	—
	✔
	✔
	—
	✔
	—

Black-chinned Hummingbird

It doesn't take a bird watcher to tell you that hummingbirds are cool. These New World specialties are understandably among the most popular birds. In the East, there is only one common hummingbird, the ruby-throated, but western North America is blessed with more than a dozen hummer species. Many of these are common in backyards. The black-chinned hummingbird is the most common and widespread hummingbird of the West, arriving on territory as early as March and frequenting woodlands and backyards throughout the summer months. The adult males of this species sport velvety black gorgets (throat feathers) accented by a gorgeous band of deep purple iridescence just below the chin.

HOW DO I IDENTIFY IT? These are average-sized hummingbirds (3¾ inches long) with the typical long, thin bill and insect-like flight style. Adult males are metallic green above and a pale grayish green below. The species is named for the adult male's dark chin that often appears all black except in certain light, when the lower throat flashes deep purple. Females and young males resemble the adult males except they lack the dark chin. Female black-chinned hummingbirds look nearly identical to the female ruby-throated hummingbird of the East, making identification tricky in the few areas where the two species both occur (mostly in Texas). Black-chinned hummingbirds do not really sing, but they are constantly uttering their distinctive *chip* calls. The males perform elaborate courtship displays that involve flying back and forth in a wide U-shaped arc.

WHERE DO I FIND IT? Look for black-chinned hummingbirds throughout the western United States between spring and summer. They show up in a wide variety of habitats, including open woodlands, oak groves, canyons, along rivers, and suburban backyards. Watch for these birds as they zip from flower to flower, or from feeder to feeder, sipping nectar.

WHAT CAN I FEED OR DO TO ATTRACT IT? Black-chinned hummingbirds are easily attracted with sugar water. For best results, mix a nectar solution of 4:1 water to white table sugar. Be sure to wash feeders with warm soapy water every few days and replace the solution. Boiling the solution briefly helps it keep longer. Artificial coloring in your hummingbird food is not necessary (most feeders have ample red parts). Sometimes a single male hummingbird can dominate a feeder, keeping other hummers from accessing the food. To thwart a bullying male, try hanging several feeders within a few feet of each other. He'll be unable to defend them all. One of the best ways to attract hummingbirds to your backyard is to plant native nectar-producing plants, such as bee balm, butterfly weed, columbine, daylily, hummingbird trumpet, and Texas sage.

NESTING Once a male hummingbird has mated, his investment in the offspring is over. The female constructs a walnut-sized, thick-walled cup of plant down and spider silk, bound tightly with elastic spider web and encrusted with lichens. This well-insulated nest protects the two pea-sized white eggs when she must leave to forage. The young hatch after about 13 days and remain in the nest for about three weeks. The female regurgitates small insects and nectar into their crops. They are fed for a week or longer after fledging. The female often begins building her next nest while still tending to the young hummers from the first.

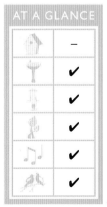

AT A GLANCE	
🏠	—
🍷	✔
🌵	✔
🕊	✔
🎵	✔
🎶	✔

Anna's Hummingbird

When you look at an adult male Anna's hummingbird in bright sunlight and he turns his head and flares his throat (gorget) feathers, your eyes are blasted with an amazing bright rose-magenta color. This 4-inch humming-bird, a year-round resident along the Pacific Coast, is our only hummingbird with bright red on both throat and crown. Fortunately, this stunning bird is common within its limited range and easily attracted to both feeders and nectar-producing flowers in backyards and gardens. In spring, males perform acrobatic courtship-display flights, spiraling more than 100 feet in the air and swooping downward twittering vocally with wings whistling to impress a female perched nearby.

HOW DO I IDENTIFY IT?   Male Anna's hummingbirds are hard to confuse with our other western hummingbirds thanks to their bright magenta throat and crown feathers. While these brightly colored feathers can appear dark at certain angles, a few moments of watching will certainly provide a flash or two of brilliant color. The backs and sides of males and females are dark green, and their bellies are smudgy greenish white. The bill is straight and medium-length. Adult females may show a few magenta feathers on the throat but look plain overall and are slightly larger than other female western hummers. The male's song is a raspy series of notes with a few squeaks in between and is often sung from an obvious perch atop a bush or small tree.

WHERE DO I FIND IT?   This is the only common hummingbird found along the Pacific Coast in winter. The Anna's hummingbird has expanded its range to the north as far as British Columbia and east into southern Arizona. In winter, some birds may move farther inland in search of food. Watch for male Anna's hummingbirds perched on top of a bare twig on a short tree or shrub. They use these as singing and territorial perches, often flying out to attack other trespassing hummers. Anna's can be found in a variety of habitats, as well as from gardens and parks to open woods, coastal scrub, streamside thickets, and chaparral, at bird feeders.

WHAT CAN I FEED OR DO TO ATTRACT IT?   Creating a healthy landscape in your backyard or garden will make it attractive to hummingbirds, all of which eat flying insects (limit the use of garden chemicals!), flower nectar, sap from tree holes drilled by sapsuckers, and nectar at feeders. Flowering plants with tube-shaped blossoms tend to be favorites among hummers for the nectar they produce on a daily basis. Add these plant families to your landscape for hummingbirds: fuchsia, chuparosa, sage, salvia, penstemon, honeysuckle, trumpet vine, columbine, larkspur, and impatiens.

Hummingbird feeders, another excellent attractant, should be cleaned regularly. Nectar, offered in a 4:1 ration of water to sugar, should be clear—red dye is not necessary.

NESTING   Female hummingbirds do all the work and the Anna's is no exception. She builds the tiny cup from spider webs and plant fibers and lays two to three eggs in it. The eggs are incubated by the female for about 20 days before hatching, and the young hummers take their first flight from the nest a bit more than three weeks later. The only role of the male Anna's is to fertilize the eggs; after that he has nothing to do with the female, nest, or offspring.

AT A GLANCE	
🏠	–
🏺	✔
🧱	✔
🪺	✔
🎵	✔
🐦	✔

Calliope Hummingbird

The Calliope (pronounced kuh-LIE-uh-pee) is the smallest bird in North America, only about three inches long and weighing only one-tenth of an ounce. These tiny birds inhabit the forests, meadows, and canyons of the northwestern United States. They frequently visit backyards with an ample supply of sugar water and nectar-producing plants. One look at this stunning green-and-magenta jewel will convince anyone that this bird is worthy of the name Calliope, the muse of epic poetry that inspired Homer to pen the Odyssey *and the* Iliad. *Though tiny, Calliope hummingbirds are capable of surviving the often chilling nights of the Rocky Mountains, where these birds nest. Calliopes are generally less aggressive than other hummer species, preferring to lay low to avoid the typical fights that occur between other hummingbirds around backyard feeders and other food sources.*

HOW DO I IDENTIFY IT? These are very small metallic-green birds. For a hummingbird, the Calliope's bill is relatively short. Adult males have metallic-green wings and back, whitish underparts, and a dazzling rosy gorget (throat feathers). While the gorget of most male hummers is a smallish patch covering the chin and throat area, the Calliope's gorget is more streaked and extends into the chest area, almost like rays. Females and young males are similar but lack the rosy throat. Males perform elaborate courtship flights in which they zip back and forth in a U-shaped arc. These flights are called "pendulum displays," and many hummer species do this to attract mates.

WHERE DO I FIND IT? Look for Calliope hummingbirds in open woodlands, mountain meadows, shrubby areas, and suburbs in the northwestern United States south to California. These birds are most common at higher elevations and in areas near water. Calliopes migrate great distances each year to their wintering grounds in Mexico, making this bird the smallest long-distance avian migrant in the world. Despite a lingering myth that seems to never go away, hummingbirds do not migrate by hitching a ride on the backs of Canada geese or any other large migratory birds. Believe it or not, these tiny travelers make the long journeys all by themselves, logging thousands of miles between their northern breeding areas and their southern wintering grounds.

WHAT CAN I FEED OR DO TO ATTRACT IT? These birds come to backyards for sugar water and flowers. For the best sugar water solution, mix one part white table sugar with four parts water, boiling the solution briefly to help it keep longer. Artificial food coloring is not necessary, as most hummer feeders have enough red parts to attract the birds. Be sure to wash your feeders with warm soapy water every few days and replace the nectar solution. Including a garden of native nectar-producing plants is another great way to lure hummers into your yard. Autumn sage, bleeding heart, columbine, hummingbird trumpet vine, azalea, and butterfly bush are all great options.

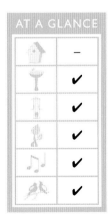

AT A GLANCE	
🏠	—
🍶	✔
🥤	✔
🌵	✔
🎵	✔
🕊	✔

NESTING As with other hummingbird species, male Calliopes are not involved with nest-building or the raising of the young. The female builds a small cup nest of plant down, held together with spider silk and camouflaged with lichens. She incubates two white eggs for about 15 days. The young leave the nest when they are about three weeks old.

Broad-tailed Hummingbird

These are fairly large hummingbirds (about 4 inches long) of the western United States and Mexico, most abundant in the mountainous areas of those regions. As you might have guessed, broad-tailed hummingbirds are named for their tails, which are slightly larger than those of other hummer species. These birds have the ability to undergo torpor, a slowed metabolic state in which the hummer's heart rate and body temperature are lowered. This allows broad-tails to endure the cold climates in which these birds often find themselves. Like other hummingbird species, broad-tails feed heavily on nectar from blooming flowers, especially red tubular flowers, and also eat a fair number of small insects. They come to backyards for both flowers and sugar water. Keep in mind that you should never use molasses or honey to make hummingbird nectar; these foods can make the birds sick.

HOW DO I IDENTIFY IT? Adult male broad-tailed hummingbirds are metallic green above and a paler, buffy green below with a deep magenta gorget (throat feathers), contrasting sharply against a nearly pure white chest. Listen for the distinctive wing-trill sound these birds make as they zip past you. Females and young males are very buffy below and have finely spotted throats without the dazzling magenta of the adult male.

WHERE DO I FIND IT? Look for these birds throughout the West, especially in mountain meadows, mixed woodlands, and canyons. During migration, broad-tailed hummingbirds show up in a wider variety of habitats, including parks and backyard gardens. Listen for the distinctive the wing trill of the adult male and also for loud chip notes.

WHAT CAN I FEED OR DO TO ATTRACT IT? Blooming, nectar-producing flowers are the best way to attract hummingbirds to your backyard. They hover and probe rapidly, zipping from flower to flower. Good hummingbird plants include various types of bee balm, butterfly weed, phlox, red morning glory, trumpet creeper, azalea, fuchsia, and hibiscus. You can also entice hummers with sugar water feeders. For best results, mix a nectar solution of four parts water to one part white table sugar. Be sure to wash hummingbird feeders with warm soapy water every few days and replace the solution. Boiling the solution briefly helps it keep longer. Adding artificial coloring to your sugar water solution is not necessary (most feeders have enough colored parts to attract the birds). Sometimes a single male hummingbird can dominate a feeder, keeping other hummers from accessing the food. To thwart a bullying male, try hanging several feeders within a few feet of each other. He'll be unable to defend them all.

NESTING The female constructs a small cup of spider webs and plant down, tightly bound with spider silk and covered with lichens, moss, and bits of bark. It typically takes her about 4 or 5 days to build the nest. These birds us a lot of spider silk during their nest construction, which is a good reason to leave old spider webs in place in spring and summer on the exterior of your home—female hummingbirds of all species are always looking for good nesting material. Two tiny white eggs are incubated for about two and a half weeks until hatching, and then the female feeds the nestlings. The young hummingbirds leave the nest when they are about three weeks old.

AT A GLANCE	
🏠	—
🗼	✔
🪶	✔
🌸	✔
🎵	✔
🐦	✔

Rufous Hummingbird

Though just 3¾ inches in length, rufous hummingbirds must think they are much bigger and stronger. They are incredibly aggressive defending a food source like blooming, nectar-producing flowers or a hummingbird feeder. Males of other hummingbird species are known to be feisty in protecting their "turf," but both male and female rufous hummingbirds behave like tiny tyrants. This species is our hardiest hummingbird, nesting as far north as Alaska and foraging in summer at super-high elevations in the Rockies when mountain meadows are full of blooming wildflowers. A very vocal hummingbird, the rufous makes a variety of buzzes and sputter notes, especially in aggressive encounters with other hummingbirds. The male's wings make a high, whining whistle in flight.

HOW DO I IDENTIFY IT? No other North American hummingbird has a rusty orange back. Though similar, the male Allen's hummingbird of coastal Oregon and California has a green back. Male rufous hummers have greenish crowns and rufous on the face, back, sides, and tail. The throat patch (gorget) flashes brilliant red in direct sunlight. The upper breast is white. Females are green on the head, back, and wings with a rusty wash on the sides. The female's tail is a colorful combination of rufous, green, and black, tipped in white. When perched, the rufous hummingbird's tail folds into a point.

WHERE DO I FIND IT? Open woods, parks, gardens, meadows, and brushy habitats—anywhere with blooming flowers and insects—are prime places to find this species. Rufous hummingbirds follow an interesting annual migration route that goes in a circle, clockwise. They breed in spring in the Pacific Northwest and head south in midsummer through the Rocky Mountains to take advantage of nectar rich meadows of wildflowers. They spend the winter primarily in Mexico, then travel up the Pacific Coast in late winter and early spring to breed in the Pacific Northwest, from Oregon and Idaho through British Columbia to southern Alaska. Over the past several decades, increasing numbers of rufous hummingbirds have spent the winter in the southeastern United States.

WHAT CAN I FEED OR DO TO ATTRACT IT? Flowering plants with tubular nectar producing blossoms (columbines, mints, penstemon, larkspurs, and currants) best attract this species. But they also consume large amounts of insects, such as gnats and flies, which they catch in flight. So take it easy on the garden chemicals if you want a hummingbird-friendly backyard. Of course, rufous hummers will also visit a hummingbird feeder filled with clear sugar water. These birds can be bullies at a nectar feeder, attacking and driving off all other visitors. But they do not stay long, so it's not necessary to do anything about it.

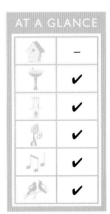

AT A GLANCE	
	–
	✔
	✔
	✔
	✔
	✔

NESTING Nesting as they do in the far Northwest, rufous hummingbirds get busy, typically producing just one brood per year. Females handle the work of nest building, incubation, brooding, and feeding the young. The role of the male is simply to fertilize the eggs. The nest is high in a tree and is built of plant down and fibers, held together by spider silk and camouflaged with bits of lichen and moss. Two or three eggs are laid and incubated for up to 17 days. Nestlings fledge about 19 days later.

Acorn Woodpecker

At first glance, you might think an acorn woodpecker was a toy bird all dolled up in clown make-up. This is certainly an odd-looking bird. But that's not all that is unique about this species. It get its name from its habit of storing acorns—a central part of its diet—in large larders, or caches, with a hole drilled in a tree trunk to hold each individual acorn. These are called granary trees and a single site may contain thousands of acorns. In areas where there are few large trees, acorn woodpeckers will sometimes resort to using wooden telephone poles and the siding on buildings for their granaries.

HOW DO I IDENTIFY IT? This medium-sized woodpecker (9 inches long) is boldly marked on the head. An acorn woodpecker looks black-backed as it hitches up a tree trunk. Adult males show a red crown, white forehead, black bill and throat, a black mask surrounding bright yellow eyes, and a necklace of yellow. The breast is white with clean streaks of black. Adult females have a smaller patch of red on the rear of the head. In flight, the acorn woodpecker shows three bright white patches on the rump and in the wings. These are very vocal birds, giving several different calls, including a burry rattle and a two-syllable call that sounds like a strange person saying *Wake up! Wake up!*

WHERE DO I FIND IT? Acorn woodpeckers are year-round residents in the oak and mixed pine-oak woodlands of the West. They are nearly always found in noisy social groups, foraging and flying from tree to tree. They often perch at the tops of trees, so they can be relatively easy to see once you locate them. A telltale sign of their presence, aside from their regular and raucous calls, is their large caches of acorns. These are amazing to look at, with each individual acorn crammed into a drilled hole. This stockpile of food is insurance against those years when the oaks produce few acorns. While the other members of a family group work to add acorns to the granary, one member is always guarding the stash.

WHAT CAN I FEED OR DO TO ATTRACT IT? Within their range and preferred oak woods habitat, acorn woodpeckers will visit bird feeders for peanuts, suet, and sunflower hearts. They will also make regular visits to a source of fresh, clean water. While they typically excavate their own nesting and roosting cavities, acorn woodpeckers will occasionally use nest boxes—particularly for roosting. One potential drawback to attracting these birds to your property is that, if your home has wooden exterior siding, acorn woodpeckers may decide to use it as a storage facility. Once this behavior starts, it can be very hard to get the birds to stop. Some backyard bird watchers have reported success in deterring woodpeckers from siding by hanging long shiny streamers or strips of bright plastic in the affected area.

NESTING A nesting cavity is excavated, along with several separate roosting cavities, and between three and six eggs are laid. Incubation lasts about 11 days and nestlings remain in the nest for a month before fledging. Offspring remain with the family group for several years, helping to raise subsequent broods and contribute to the storage of acorns.

Downy Woodpecker

Downy woodpeckers are a favorite of backyard bird watchers because they are often the first woodpeckers to visit bird feeders. Common in any habitat with trees, downies are equally at home in backyards and in remote woods. In all seasons, downy woodpeckers give a rattling whinny that descends in tone. They also utter a sharp pik! *call regularly while foraging. Downy woodpeckers use their stiff tails and strong, clawed feet to propel themselves along tree branches or trunks.*

HOW DO I IDENTIFY IT?   The downy is the smallest (6¾ inches long), most common, and most widespread North American woodpecker. Its black-and-white plumage is similar to that of the larger (9¼ inches long) hairy woodpecker. Telling the downy and hairy woodpecker apart can be difficult. In both species, the males have a red patch at the back of the head. Downy woodpeckers have an all-white breast and belly and a white stripe down the middle of their back. The wings and tail are black with white spots. A way to remember which is which is: downy is dinky; hairy is huge. Downies have a small body, a small head, and a small, thin bill. Hairies have a big body, a big head, and a large, chisel-like bill.

WHERE DO I FIND IT?   A common resident of woodlands throughout North America, the downy is a habitat generalist—found anywhere there are trees or woody plants on which to find food. Though their population appears stable, downies suffer from nest site competition from other cavity nesters and from the removal of dead trees, which they need for nesting and feeding. Look for them along the edges of woods, hitching along smaller branches, pecking and drilling for their insect-based food items. The sounds downy woodpeckers make while foraging as well as their frequent vocalizations are often the first clue to their presence.

WHAT CAN I FEED OR DO TO ATTRACT IT?   Downy woodpeckers probe and chisel at a tree's bark searching for insects, insect eggs, ants, and spiders. They also eat fruits, such as sumac and poison ivy. At bird feeders, sunflower seeds, suet, peanuts, and peanut butter are favorites. They use a variety of feeder types, including hopper, tube, satellite, and suet designs. They occasionally visit hummingbird feeders for a sip of nectar. Though downies rarely nest in nest boxes, they readily use them for nighttime roosting, especially in harsh weather. If you have nest boxes for bluebirds or swallows, consider leaving them up year-round. In areas of cold winter temperatures, plug the ventilation holes with moldable weather-stripping. Leave a dead tree or large dead branch on a tree in your yard (in a safe location) and you will be much more likely to attract woodpeckers.

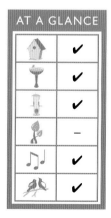

AT A GLANCE	
🏠	✔
🕊	✔
🗼	✔
🌹	–
♫	✔
🐦	✔

NESTING   Like all woodpeckers, downies are cavity nesters. Each spring they excavate a new nest hole in the dead stub or trunk of a tree—usually one that is already rotting. The nest hole is placed underneath an overhanging branch higher than 12 feet above the ground. Excavation can take as long as two weeks—even with the male and female participating. Clutch size is usually four to five white eggs, which both sexes incubate. Hatching occurs at 12 days, and both parents feed the young for about three weeks until they fledge.

Hairy Woodpecker

A familiar visitor to bird feeders, the hairy woodpecker is named for the long, hairlike white feathers on its back. The hairy looks like a super-sized version of a downy woodpecker, but the best way to tell these two similar species apart is to compare the length of the bill to the length of the head (front to back). The hairy's bill is always longer than the width of its head, and the downy's bill is always shorter than the length of its head. An easier way to remember is: downy is dinky; hairy is huge.

HOW DO I IDENTIFY IT? Hairy woodpeckers are medium-sized woodpeckers (9¼ inches long) with a long, sturdy, chisel-like bill that is used for finding food, for excavating nest holes, and for territorial drumming on hollow trees. Males and females look the same, with white bellies, a white central back stripe, and distinctly patterned black and white on faces and wings. Adult males, however, have a red patch at the back of the head. Hairies utter a sharp *peek!* call, as well as a loud ringing rattle on a single pitch.

WHERE DO I FIND IT? Hairy woodpeckers are year-round residents across North America in mature forests and wherever there are large trees, including suburban backyards, urban parks, and isolated woodlots. If your neighborhood has large shade trees or mature woods, chances are good that you've got hairy woodpeckers nearby. Check large, dead snags and branches for woodpecker holes and listen for the birds' vocalizations and drumming in spring. They are one of our most widespread woodpeckers, with a range extending into Central America.

WHAT CAN I FEED OR DO TO ATTRACT IT? Using their bills, hairy woodpeckers can glean insects from tree bark or excavate them from beneath the bark's surface. Primary diet items include beetles, spiders, moth larvae, and ants, as well as fruits, seeds, and nuts. Offer peanuts, sunflower seeds, or suet (in winter) in hanging feeders to attract hairy woodpeckers to your yard. They will also be attracted to large dead trees or snags, especially if these are placed or occur naturally partway between the cover of a woodlot and your bird feeders. Hairies use these snag perches as a stopping point from which to check to see if the coast is clear before swooping in to visit your feeders.

NESTING It can take up to three weeks for a pair of hairy woodpeckers to excavate their nest cavity in the trunk or dead branch of a living tree. When completed, the nest cavity will have a 2-inch entry hole and will be 4 inches wide and as deep as 16 inches. Into this cozy space, four eggs are laid, and both parents share the roughly two-week incubation period. Less than a month after hatching, young hairies are ready to fledge from the nest, though the parents tend them for several more weeks. In spring and summer, watch for the recently fledged young woodpeckers following the adults to your feeding station, where they beg to be fed. A new nest is excavated each spring, but old cavities are used for roosting at night and in winter.

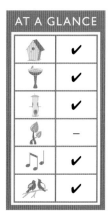

AT A GLANCE

🏠	✔
🛁	✔
🗼	✔
🌿	–
🎵	✔
🐦	✔

Northern Flicker

A familiar and fairly large woodpecker (13 inches long), the northern flicker is a distinctively marked bird that—unlike other woodpeckers—is often seen foraging on the ground. The eastern form of the flicker is known as the yellow-shafted flicker for its bright lemon-yellow underwing and tail color. A red-shafted form of the northern flicker occurs in the West. There are more than 130 different names by which the flicker is known, including high-hole, yellowhammer, and yawkerbird.

HOW DO I IDENTIFY IT?   The northern flicker is all field marks with its bright yellow wing flashes, white rump, spotted breast, and barred back. It is not easily confused with any other bird. In the East, both sexes have a red crescent on the back of the head, but only males show a black "moustache" mark on the cheek. In the West, the red-shafted form of the northern flicker lacks the red crescent on the back of the head, but males show a red moustache. The flicker has several calls, including a single-note *kleer,* a short *wickawicka* series, and a monotonous *wickwickwickwick* song. It also communicates by drumming on the resonating surface of trees, poles, or even metal downspouts and chimney flues.

WHERE DO I FIND IT?   The northern flicker is found almost everywhere wooded habitats exist, though open woods and woodland edges are preferred. Look for them foraging on open, grassy areas and along sidewalks, especially where there are any colonies. In their swooping, undulating flight they are hard to ignore as they flash a white rump, a brown back barred with black, and either golden-yellow or pinkish-red underwings. Flickers in the northern portion of the range migrate southward in winter, while southern birds are nonmigratory.

WHAT CAN I FEED OR DO TO ATTRACT IT?   Flickers love ants. A flicker pokes its long bill into an anthill and uses its long, sticky tongue to extract the ants. They also eat other insects, as well as fruits and seeds. Offering suet, corn, sunflower seeds, grapes, or peanuts at your feeders or hung on large trees will be attractive to flickers. Providing nest boxes in your wooded backyard is another way to attract them. Equally important is the presence of ground-dwelling insects (leave those non-threatening anthills alone!) and dead trees or dead branches. A large, dead tree branch placed vertically in your yard may entice a flicker to stop and check out your other offerings.

NESTING   Northern flickers excavate a new nest cavity almost every year. In doing so, they perform a much-needed service for many other hole-nesting birds—from chickadees to ducks—that use old flicker nests because they lack the strong bills and ability to excavate their own nesting cavities. Both male and female flickers excavate the nest cavity in a dead tree or branch. The female lays five to ten eggs; both sexes share the 11-day incubation period. Young flickers leave the nest after about 25 days. Flickers will use nest boxes with an interior floor of 7 × 7 inches, an interior height of 16 to 24 inches, and a 2½-inch entry hole. Because excavation is a vital part of courtship, boxes packed full of woodchips are more attractive. Competition for cavities from European starlings is fierce and may be causing a decline in flickers.

AT A GLANCE	
🏠	✔
⛲	✔
🌿	✔
🌸	–
♪♩	✔
🐦🐦	✔

Gray Jay

Often compared to an oversized chickadee, gray jays are familiar residents of the far North. Next to the bright and colorful blue jay of the East, the striking green jay of southern Texas and Mexico, or even the black-and-blue Steller's jay of the West, the gray jay is drably colored with an overall grayish plumage. But what these birds lack in brilliant plumage they more than make up for with bold personalities. Gray jays will watch for unsuspecting hikers along forest trails and then quietly follow them through the woods, often going completely unnoticed until the birds make their move. The jays boldly invade picnic areas, campsites, and cabins to snatch bread, peanuts, raisins, or just about anything else they can get their beaks on. This practice has earned them the nickname "Camp Robber," among other names.

HOW DO I IDENTIFY IT?   These are fairly large birds (about 11½ inches long) with long tails; relatively short, dark bills; and no crests. Adults are grayish overall, with dark gray above and light gray below. They have varying amounts of dark gray on their heads. Young gray jays are dark gray overall with white marking on their faces. They retain this plumage for the first few months of their lives. Listen for their harsh calls, which include a distinctive screech that sounds like a blue jay imitation. Similar species include northern and loggerhead shrikes (smaller birds with conspicuous black masks) and the Clark's nutcracker (slightly larger with a noticeably longer bill).

WHERE DO I FIND IT?   Chances are that these birds will find you first. Gray jays are year-round residents throughout the northern boreal forests of Canada. In the United States, these birds are found in Alaska, the Northwest, mountainous areas of California and the Interior West, and the northernmost New England states. You are most likely to find gray jays in forests, especially spruce and fir forests, but you can also look for them in bogs and mixed woodlands. They are commonly encountered near hiking trails, camping sites, ski lodges, picnic areas, and backyards. Gray jays do not regularly migrate, but during winter they will sometimes move south into new areas where they do not normally occur, looking for food.

WHAT CAN I FEED OR DO TO ATTRACT IT?   These birds will eat just about anything, and they are likely to come to you looking for handouts before you even set anything out. Gray jays will eat most of the typical feeder offerings but are especially fond of suet. They will also take meat scraps, bread, peanuts, and raisins. Despite their large size, they will come to tube feeders as well as platform or ground feeders. Because they are so tame and bold, gray jays will often come and eat directly from your hand.

NESTING   Gray jays nest very early, often during late winter in cold, snowy conditions. Both parents build a bulky nest of twigs, bark strips, and lichens, usually lined with animal hair or feathers. The female incubates three or four pale greenish eggs that are marked with brownish or reddish spots. Incubation typically lasts about three weeks, and then both parents feed the nestlings. The young leave the nest after about three weeks but stay with their parents for an additional month before moving out on their own.

AT A GLANCE	
🏠	—
🛁	✔
🗼	✔
🌿	—
🎵	✔
🐦	—

Steller's Jay

Jays are smart, adaptable, and noisy birds. They will often mimic the call of a red-tailed or red-shouldered hawk as they approach a bird feeder in an apparent attempt to scare other birds away from the food. An interesting story surrounds the initial discovery of this bird. In 1741, a German naturalist by the name of Georg Steller spent a single day in Alaska with an exploration team from nearby Russia. While there, Steller noticed many unfamiliar species, including this handsome black-and-blue jay. He recognized the bird as a relative of the blue jay (as depicted in paintings) from eastern North America. This led to the crew's conclusion that they had indeed arrived in America.

HOW DO I IDENTIFY IT? These are fairly large birds (about 11 inches long) birds with long tails, large, dark bills, and conspicuous black crests. Steller's jays are very dark overall, a unique characteristic among jay species, with a jet-black upper half and deep blue lower half. Males and females look alike, but there is quite a bit of geographic variability in plumage; Steller's jays along the Pacific coast are noticeably darker overall than eastern birds. In fact, scientists have described up to sixteen different subspecies of the Steller's jay. These birds occasionally interbreed with the blue jay of the East where the two species' ranges overlap just east of the Rocky Mountains. You can pick jays out on the wing by their unique, swooping flight, often in small groups flying in single file.

WHERE DO I FIND IT? This is the most common and widespread jay of the West. You will find this species in coniferous and mixed pine-oak forests throughout much of western North America, from southern Alaska south to the Mexican border. Steller's jays are especially common in mountainous areas. They generally do not migrate, remaining in the same areas year-round. Steller's jays frequent backyards, parks, and campsites where they hope to score some handouts. These are noisy birds; listen for their harsh, raspy cries or their stellar (pardon the pun) rendition of a red-shouldered hawk's call.

WHAT CAN I FEED OR DO TO ATTRACT IT? Jays will eat almost anything, and this species is no exception. Away from feeders, Steller's jays usually eat pine nuts, acorns, berries, and fruits. They supplement their summer diet with a wide variety of spiders and insects, including wasps and bees. Sometimes they'll even eat the young and eggs of other birds, small rodents, and lizards. Steller's jays are easily enticed to visit backyards with suet, peanuts and nuts, sunflower seeds, cracked corn, and even dog food. Jays are able to handle peanuts still in the shell. These birds are also attracted to a reliable source of clean, moving water for drinking and bathing.

NESTING Steller's jays nest in woodlands, parks, and backyards, sometimes even in urban areas. Though both sexes help gather materials, females handle most of the nest construction. The bulky nest is made of plant fibers, dry leaves, moss, and sticks mixed with mud. Pine needles and animal hair usually line the nest. The female lays four or five bluish green eggs one day at a time, incubating them for about 16 days. The parents feed the young for another 16 days until the young birds are ready leave the nest.

AT A GLANCE	
🏠	—
⚱	✔
🕯	✔
🌻	✔
🎵	✔
🐦	—

Western Scrub-Jay

The western scrub-jay is found in dry lowlands, wooded hillsides, and scrub oak forests of the West. Its loud shack-shack-shack-shack *call reverberates as pairs of these raucous birds move about the scrub habitat for which they are named. There are three separate scrub-jay species in North America, but only the western scrub-jay, the blue-colored jay of the West, is widespread and common. They other two, the Florida scrub-jay and island scrub-jay, have very small populations and limited ranges. Western scrub-jays are incredibly creative when seeking food. They will beg at picnic tables, steal acorns from the granaries of acorn woodpeckers, and perch on the backs of mule deer to remove and eat the tasty ticks they find there.*

HOW DO I IDENTIFY IT? The western scrub-jay is a medium-sized jay at just over 11 inches in length. Its long tail gives it a slender look. In flight, they appear flopping and slow on rounded wings and are usually seen in small flocks. The scrub-jay is deep blue on the crown, neck, wings, and tail. There is a dark mask around the eyes and a thin white eyeline above. The upper back is gray and the wings and tail are deep blue. A faintly streaked white throat and plain gray belly complete the scrub-jay's plumage. Unlike the blue jay of the eastern two-thirds of North America, this species is crestless. Another common jay of the West is the Steller's jay, which is darker overall with an obvious black head and crest. Western scrub-jays make a variety of sounds—all of them harsh, rasping, and loud.

WHERE DO I FIND IT? Scrub-jays are obvious, noisy, and colorful birds. This species is most common in areas where scrub oaks, pinyons, and junipers are the dominant trees, though they can be found almost anywhere there is scrubby, brushy habitat, including suburban parks and backyards. Flocks of scrub-jays are a common sight as they fly across an open area or roadway in ones and twos. As a flock forages—often on or near the ground—one or more scrub-jays will remain perched up high, serving as a lookout. Wherever they occur, western scrub-jays are year-round residents, though in harsh winter weather or in times of limited natural food supplies, birds living at higher elevations may move to the lowlands.

WHAT CAN I FEED OR DO TO ATTRACT IT? In the West, any backyard with scrub oaks, pinyons, or juniper trees may have a visit from a flock of scrub-jays. In summer, their diet is largely insects, while the fall and winter diet shifts to fruits, seeds, and nuts. They will visit bird feeders for sunflower seeds, peanuts, suet or suet dough, and other offerings. A reliable source of water is another good attractant. If your property includes scrubby habitat with good cover and a reliable food supply, you may entice a pair of western scrub-jays to nest.

NESTING Scrub-jays build their nests relatively low in a tree or shrub, with males and females contributing to its construction. The cup-shaped nest is made of twigs, rootlets, grass, and other plants and may be lined with animal fur. Between three to seven eggs are laid and incubated by the female for about 16 days. Young scrub-jays stay in the nest for a bit more than two weeks before fledging.

AT A GLANCE	
🏠	—
🛁	✔
🗼	✔
🍃	✔
🎵	✔
🐦	—

American Crow

The American crow is our most widespread and common member of the corvid family, which includes crows, ravens, jays, and magpies. Noisy, sly, opportunistic, and ubiquitous, the American crow lives among us, yet comparatively little is known about it. Like other bold, brash members of the corvid family (the blue jay being a prime example), the crow is downright sneaky where its personal life is concerned. Few people know that crows may breed cooperatively in groups of up to a dozen birds, helping tend the dominant pair's nest. Loud, bordering on obnoxious, most of the year, crows are incredibly quiet during nesting.

HOW DO I IDENTIFY IT? American crows are glossy black from bill to toenail. They are armed with a stout, strong bill that acts as a chisel, axe, shovel, or forceps, among other uses. The crow's distinctive wing beats appear to row the bird through the sky. Crows are well known for their raucous caw. Evidence from field studies suggests that crows have different "words" for different situations (flock assembly, dispersal, mobbing); their language is complex, as is their social behavior. Few are privileged to hear the crow's song, given by both sexes, which is a long recitation of rattles, coos, growls, and imitations of sounds. The common raven is a larger, stockier relative of the American crow. In flight, ravens show a wedge-shaped tail—crows show a square-ended tail. Ravens are as common as crows in parts of the West, in the far North, and in the eastern mountains. In the coastal Southeast the smaller, more nasal-sounding fish crow can be confused with the American crow.

WHERE DO I FIND IT? Though they are strongly associated with farmland and open areas with scattered woodlots, crows find perfect conditions in cities and suburbs, where they raid pet dishes, bird feeders, and garbage cans. In the northern part of their range, crows are migratory, but all American crows spend the winter within the continental United States. Throughout their range, when not breeding, crows gather into large roosts, and these can swell to thousands of birds by late winter.

WHAT CAN I FEED OR DO TO ATTRACT IT? Crows are always up to something, and feeding them gives us an opportunity to observe their always-intriguing behavior. To find something a crow might like, open the refrigerator. Freezer-burned meat is a favorite. Cracked or whole corn is irresistible as well. Neighbors may wonder, but crows are well worth watching. There's almost nothing edible an American crow will not eat. At roadkills, landfills, and compost piles, crows will load their distensible throat with food and fly heavily off, often caching it under leaves or sod for later enjoyment. Crows forage by walking slowly on the ground—hunting invertebrates and vertebrates alike—and are constantly scanning roadsides and fields as they fly, descending to investigate anything that might be edible.

NESTING Crows stay in family units composed of parents and their young from the previous year. These yearlings may help build the nest, incubate, or feed the incubating female or her young. Four or five eggs are laid in the bulky twig nest, which is usually hidden high in a pine. The female incubates for around 17 days, and young fledge at around 36 days. Their strangled, nasal calls sometimes betray the nest location.

AT A GLANCE	
🏠	–
(bird bath)	✔
(feeder)	✔
(flower)	–
♫	✔
(birds)	–

Tree Swallow

The lovely tree swallow is expanding its breeding range into the southern United States. Elsewhere, it's established and common in spring and summer (with the exception of the most arid regions and habitats). Previously limited by the availability of their required nesting cavities, tree swallows benefit greatly from artificial nest boxes erected to attract eastern bluebirds. Their liquid twittering, sharp blue-and-white color, and trusting ways make them welcome in your backyard. Before the advent of artificial nest boxes, tree swallows nested in old woodpecker holes—a hotly contested resource. Scores of birds, other animals, and even bees and wasps may be contending for a limited number of old woodpecker holes.

HOW DO I IDENTIFY IT? Long, triangular wings, snowy white under-parts, and glossy teal blue upperparts make the tree swallow a beautiful signal of spring. Soaring kitelike, then rising with rapid flaps, they course and dive over meadows and ponds in their search for flying insects. Their jingling calls have been likened to the sound of someone shaking paperclips in a tumbler. Females are somewhat browner above and a duller blue than males. Juvenile birds are brown-backed and white below.

WHERE DO I FIND IT? Tree swallows prefer open fields, preferably near water, for nesting, though they will inhabit upland sites. Marshes—fresh and salt—provide the flying insects they require. The tree swallow's breeding habitat extends across Canada and the northern tier of the United States and is rapidly expanding into the Southeast. Tree swallows winter in coastal areas from South Carolina to Florida and along the Gulf Coast into Mexico and Central America. They are found year-round in much of central and southern California. In late summer, tree swallows gather in large pre-migratory flocks sometimes numbering thousands. They migrate in small flocks, with many birds heading as far south as Central America. Others remain in the coastal United States, eating fruits when cold weather kills flying insects.

WHAT CAN I FEED OR DO TO ATTRACT IT? Eighty percent of its diet is insects; fruits make up the rest, mainly bayberries that sustain it in adverse winter weather. This ability to eat fruit helps tree swallows out-live cold snaps as they make their way northward to breed. Insects are caught on the wing in spectacular zigzag flights and are stored in the throat to be fed to nestlings. Allowing your property to naturally produce flying insects will attract tree swallows. The very best way to attract them is to erect nest boxes with a 1⁹⁄₁₆-inch hole, mounted on a predator-proof pole in an open meadow near water; it's virtually guaranteed to catch the attention of a passing tree swallow. Get the housing up early in spring, since tree swallows are often the first of our swallows to return.

NESTING A foundation of coarse grass, leaves, and stems is lined with large body feathers, usually white. Tree swallows are mad for feathers in nesting season and can often be induced to take soft white feathers from your hand. A New York study showed that eggs hatched and nestlings survived better in nests insulated with more feathers. The female incubates four to seven eggs for an average of 14 days. Young leave the nest 15 to 25 days later, flying strongly. Second broods are rare, but seem to be more frequent in the South.

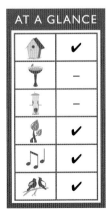

AT A GLANCE

🏠	✔
🛁	–
🪶	–
🌿	✔
♪♩	✔
🐦🐦	✔

Violet-green Swallow

This small swallow of the West is aptly named: the glimmering, dark feathers on its back can appear green, blue, violet, and even bronze-colored in bright, direct sunlight. Like other swallows, the violet-green forages in flight, catching flying insects with its bill. These birds are tireless, expert flyers and will regularly range far from their nesting location as they forage during daylight. When they mix with other swallow species and swifts, violet-green swallows are often the highest-flying birds, swooping after insects far above the others.

HOW DO I IDENTIFY IT? The adult male violet-green swallow is greenish blue above and white below. It's quite similar in appearance to the tree swallow, which is found all across North America. The violet-green can be identified by a bold crescent of white on the side of the face and by the pair of white patches that nearly meet on the dark rump. These white areas are easy to see, especially on flying birds. Tree swallows, by contrast, have an all-dark face and rump. Seen together, the violet-green swallow appears smaller, and greener on the back than the tree swallow, which has a dark blue back. Female and immature violet-green swallows are less colorful above with faces that appear dirty, or less cleanly white.

WHERE DO I FIND IT? This swallow can be found almost anywhere in the West in spring and summer (they winter in Mexico). They nest in open forests and on wooded mountainsides but can also commonly nest in towns and on treeless prairies provided there is a steady supply of flying insects and cavities in which to nest. Flocks of swallows seen flying high in the sky over mountains or mountain canyons are almost certainly violet-green swallows. Nest boxes placed along rural roads in western North America for western or mountain bluebirds are used, instead, by violet-green swallows.

WHAT CAN I FEED OR DO TO ATTRACT IT? The natural bounty of flying insect life that an open, healthy habitat produces will be the surest way to attract violet-green swallows wherever they occur in the West. Scan the sky above your property during the warmer months when you notice a hatch of midges, winged ants, moths, or other swallow prey. The next best way to attract them is to place nest boxes in an appropriate habitat. Swallows like to nest in standard bluebird nest boxes, with an entrance hole that is 1½ inches in diameter. In areas where snakes, raccoons, and other climbing predators are common, mount the housing on a pole with a predator baffle beneath it. If you have swallows nesting in or near your backyard, try tossing a few white craft feathers in the air. They may swoop down to catch them and steal them away for use in the nest.

NESTING This species will nest in any cavity available to it, from old woodpecker holes to nest boxes to small crevices in rocky cliff faces. They cannot excavate their own cavities, however, so they are easy to lure to nest boxes. Inside the cavity, the violet-green swallow builds a shallow cup of grass and rootlets and lines it with feathers. Four to six eggs are incubated by the female for two weeks or slightly longer, but the young swallows do not leave the nest until about 24 days later. After leaving the nest, the young are fed by the adults several weeks.

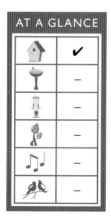

AT A GLANCE	
🏠	✔
(bird bath)	–
(feeder)	–
(plant)	–
♪♩	–
(birds)	–

Barn Swallow

The barn swallow is named for its preferred nesting location of barns. This species seems to define what it means to be at home in the air. One early naturalist estimated that a barn swallow that lived ten years would fly more than two million miles, enough to travel eighty-seven times around the earth. One of the most familiar and beloved birds in rural America, the barn swallow is welcomed everywhere as a sign of spring. Nothing says "country" more than a pair of barn swallows zipping in and out of the open doors of a working barn, darting after insects and chattering incessantly. Sometimes two or three pairs will share a favored site during nesting season. They ignore the normal activity of the people and animals that regularly use the barn, but if a strange person or animal approaches, the adults will swoop and chatter and snap their bills at the trespasser.

HOW DO I IDENTIFY IT? Glossy blue-black above and orange below, the barn swallow is the only American swallow that has a true "swallow tail," with an elongated outer pair of tail feathers forming a deep V. The females are not quite as glossy or highly colored, and the fork in their tails is not quite as pronounced. Like all swallows, they have short legs and rather weak feet used for perching, not walking. They are much more graceful in flight than on the ground. The similar-looking cliff swallow prefers to nest on rocky cliffs and under bridges, as its name suggests. It is not as common around human habitation as is the barn swallow. The cliff swallow shows a pale tan forehead and rump and lacks the barn swallow's deeply notched tail.

WHERE DO I FIND IT? The barn swallow may be found over any open area, such as pastures, fields, and golf courses, as well as lakes, ponds, and rivers. It has adapted well to humans and is not shy of people, nesting close to settled areas as long as it has open space for feeding. Barn swallows travel in great flocks during migrations, often in company with other swallow species. They arrive in most of their U.S. range in April and leave in early to mid-fall.

WHAT CAN I FEED OR DO TO ATTRACT IT? Foraging almost entirely on the wing, the barn swallow takes a variety of insect prey, from flies and locusts to moths, grasshoppers, bees, and wasps. Occasionally small berries or seeds are eaten, but this is uncommon. Only in bad weather will barn swallows feed on the ground. During breeding season, you may bring barn swallows into close range by throwing white feathers into the air near a flock of soaring birds; the graceful fliers will swoop in to snatch them up to use for nest linings. Barn swallows also enjoy eating bits of baked eggshells during breeding season. Bake the shells at 250° Fahrenheit for 20 minutes to sterilize them, then crumble into small bits and sprinkle on the ground.

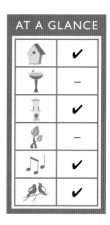

AT A GLANCE

🏠	✔
⛲	–
🪶	✔
🌿	–
🎵	✔
🐦🐦	✔

NESTING The barn swallow's nest is a cup of mud and grass, lined with feathers and placed on a rafter or glued under an eave. Besides barns, other open buildings, covered porches, or the undersides of bridges or docks are used. During second nestings, immatures from the first brood help feed and care for their younger siblings.

Black-capped Chickadee

The familiar black-capped chickadee is a year-round resident throughout Canada and the northern half of the United States. Chickadees travel in noisy little bands and draw attention to themselves with their frequent scolding chatter. In winter, their flock-mates may include titmice, nuthatches, wrens, creepers, kinglets, and other species. Chickadees are often the first birds to discover a newly installed bird feeder. In the southeastern United States, the resident chickadee is actually the Carolina chickadee, a slightly smaller but otherwise quite similar cousin of the black-capped. Fortunately, confusing these two species is rarely an issue in the West, as the Carolina does not normally occur west of Texas or Oklahoma.

HOW DO I IDENTIFY IT? Both chickadees have black caps and bibs as well as white cheek patches; gray backs, wings, and tails; and pale underparts with buff-colored flanks. The bill is tiny and dark, and the legs and feet are black.

Males and females are alike, and there are no seasonal differences in plumage. In general, black-capped chickadees are larger (5¼ inches long), bigger-headed, with brighter white cheeks. Carolina chickadees are drabber gray overall, smaller (4¾ inches long), with less white in the wings. Vocal clues can be helpful. Black-cappeds sing *fee-bee* (two notes) while Carolinas sing *soo-fee, soo-fay* (four notes). The common *chick-a-dee-dee-dee* call is lower, hoarser, and slower from black-cappeds, and higher and more melodic from Carolinas.

WHERE DO I FIND IT?   Black-capped chickadees prefer open deciduous woods with oaks, willows, birches, and alders among their favored trees. This species is resident (nonmigratory) and through most of its range it is the only chickadee present. It is generally replaced by the Carolina chickadee in the southern half of the midwestern states. The dividing line between the ranges of our two widespread chickadee species runs from central New Jersey, west through Pennsylvania, Ohio, Indiana, Illinois, Missouri, Kansas, Oklahoma, and Texas. North of this line it's mostly black-capped chickadees; south of it, primarily Carolina chickadees. Where the two species overlap they may occasionally interbreed, so identifying individual birds under such circumstances is tricky. Black-cappeds will occasionally move south in winter.

WHAT CAN I FEED OR DO TO ATTRACT IT?   Chickadees have a varied diet. Nearly half of the food taken in the wild consists of insects, such as aphids, ants, moths, and leafhoppers. They also eat spiders, weed seeds, and the seeds and small fruits of many trees (maples, oaks, birches) and vines such as grapes, Virginia creeper, and honeysuckle. It is easy to lure chickadees into your yard by providing black-oil sunflower seed in hanging tubes or hopper feeders, and by offering suet or other fats, such as a peanut butter-cornmeal mix or "bird pudding." They also enjoy peanuts, mealworms, and a reliable source of clean water. To induce a pair to stay and nest, install one or more nest boxes with entrance holes that are 1¼ to 1½ inches in diameter.

NESTING   Cavity nesters, black-capped chickadees seek out natural holes in woodland trees, often adapting old woodpecker holes. They readily accept not only nesting boxes, but also crevices under eaves or porch roofs, hollowed-out fence posts, or drainpipes. The nest (made by the female) is a thick mass of mosses, bark, and grasses, enclosing a cup of soft hair. One side is built up higher than the other and can be pulled down like a flap to cover the young when both parents are away. As many as eight eggs are laid and incubated by the female for 11 to 13 days; both parents then share the feeding of the young until they fledge after two weeks.

AT A GLANCE	
🏠	✔
(bird bath)	✔
(feeder)	✔
(utensils)	—
♫	✔
(birds)	—

Mountain Chickadee

A common and widespread bird in the forests of the mountain West, the mountain chickadee prefers to live in or near conifers. Like its chickadee relatives, the mountain chickadee is active and noisy as it forages high in the tall trees, often in mixed flocks with other species. These tagalong chickadee friends probably benefit from the mountain chickadee's inquisitive nature while foraging and its watchfulness in avoiding predators and danger. Mountain chickadees forage by gleaning insects and spiders from tree branches and bark. They also will hang upside-down like tiny acrobats to pry seeds from pine and spruce cones, and they regularly hover to glean insects from the undersides of branches and leaves.

HOW DO I IDENTIFY IT?   The mountain chickadee looks very similar to the much more widespread black-capped chickadee, but it has a single white line—like an eyebrow—over the eye and a black line below that, through the eye. This gives the mountain chickadee a masked look. Males and females look alike. These are very active birds and are more easily heard before they are seen, since they prefer to live in forests of large evergreen trees. Their *chick-a-dee-dee-dee* call sounds a bit more hoarse than a black-capped chickadee's. The mountain's song is a series of three or four notes: *fee-fee-bee* with the first note being higher pitched than the last two or three.

WHERE DO I FIND IT?   As its name suggests, this is a bird of the mountains, ranging from western Canada south through the Rocky Mountains to west Texas, New Mexico, and Arizona and west to California. It nests at high elevations and may move to lower elevations in winter, though this is a year-round resident across most of the range. Mountain chickadees are nearly always found near conifers—spruce, fir, pine, pinyon, juniper—as well as aspen groves. Watch for mountain chickadees foraging in mixed-species flocks during fall, winter, and spring.

WHAT CAN I FEED OR DO TO ATTRACT IT?   Plantings of the conifer tree species listed above may attract this species. During the nesting season in late spring and summer, they may choose to excavate a nest in the soft wood of aspen or birch trees. They will use nest boxes as well as old woodpecker holes for nesting, so leaving dead trees in place where it is safe to do so can enhance your bird-friendly habitat. Their diet during spring and summer is largely insects, spiders, and berries. In fall and winter, they shift to seeds. Within their range, mountain chickadees can become regular visitors to bird feeders, where they prefer sunflower seeds and hearts, peanut bits, suet, and suet dough. And a source of clean water in a birdbath or water feature always attracts chickadees.

NESTING   Both males and females will work to excavate or enlarge a nesting cavity in soft wood and to build the nest inside, which is made out of fibers of bark, plants, grasses, moss, and animal fur or bird feathers. As many as a dozen eggs will be laid and incubated by the female for about two weeks. Nestlings are fed a diet of insects and spiders by both parents for about three weeks before fledging. If a nest is disturbed, the incubating female or nestlings may hiss like a snake to discourage predators!

AT A GLANCE

	✔
	✔
	✔
	✔
	✔
	—

Chestnut-backed Chickadee

These multicolored chickadees are common within their limited range of western Canada and the northwestern United States. In certain parts of the humid coastal areas of the Northwest, this is the only chickadee species you are likely to encounter. These birds have rich, chestnut-colored backs and sides, the rest of their plumage being black, gray, and white. Chestnut-backed chickadees have that characteristic black cap and bib like most other chicka-dee species. Watch for flocks of these birds in forests and other wooded areas, especially in the treetops, where they actively forage for insects, seeds, and berries, often hanging upside-down as they glean for food. They're usually in the company of other small birds, including titmice, nuthatches, and other chickadees. Chestnut-backed chickadees commonly visit suburban backyards for seeds and suet.

HOW DO I IDENTIFY IT? These are small birds (4¾ inches long), about the same size and shape of our other chickadee species. What sets these birds apart is the extensive rust coloration on the back and sides. Our other western chickadees—black-capped and mountain—are only gray, black, and white. Males and females look alike. Chestnut-backed chickadees sing a unique song consisting of fast, thin notes, quite different from the whistled songs of other chickadees. They also frequently utter a loud *chick-a-dee* call.

WHERE DO I FIND IT? You will find these birds in the humid coastal and interior forests of the westernmost parts of North America, from southern Alaska to southern California. These birds are expanding their range to include more suburban areas in California, becoming more common in cities like San Francisco. Chestnut-backed chickadees are resident throughout their range, meaning they don't migrate. Listen for their calls and focus on the tops of tall trees these birds most frequently forage.

WHAT CAN I FEED OR DO TO ATTRACT IT? These birds have a varied diet. Away from feeders, chestnut-backed chickadees eat a wide variety of insects, including leafhoppers, aphids, wasps, beetles, caterpillars, and moths. They also feed on seeds, berries, and fruit. You can bring them to your yard by offering hanging tubes or hopper feeders full of sunflower seeds, other mixed seeds, and suet. These birds are also attracted to clean, moving water in a birdbath or other water feature. You can encourage chestnut-backed chickadees to nest in your backyard by installing one or more nest boxes. These boxes should be placed along woodland edges or just inside the woods and should have an entrance hole between 1⅛ and 1½ inches in diameter.

NESTING These birds nest either in man-made nest boxes or in natural tree cavities, usually about 10 feet above the ground, but sometimes higher. The chestnut-backed chickadees often return to use the same nesting site for more than one year. Their nests are made of moss, grass, lichens, bark, and animal fur. One side is built up higher than the other and can be pulled down like a flap to cover it if the female is away foraging. The female incubates anywhere from one to eleven white eggs, usually marked with reddish brown spots. The eggs hatch after about two weeks of incubation, and both parents feed the nestlings until fledging, which occurs when the young are about three weeks old.

AT A GLANCE	
🏠	✔
🛁	✔
🗼	✔
🌱	✔
🎵	✔
🐦	–

Oak & Juniper Titmouse

These two species were once considered a single species: the plain titmouse. Over time, field studies revealed their natural differences and they were split into two species, each one named for the kind of trees with which it is closely associated. The name "plain titmouse" was also appropriate because these two birds lack any notable field marks beyond their crested heads and mousy black eyes. Both species are lively, active birds, moving about their year-round habitats in small family groups sweetly calling to and scolding one another as they forage for insects, nuts, and seeds. The oak titmouse is pictured.

HOW DO I IDENTIFY IT? Both of these timice are small creatures, measuring just 5¾ inches in length. Plain gray overall with an obvious crest on the head, both of these titmice are a darker shade of gray above and paler below. The oak titmouse is slightly browner overall than the juniper titmouse, but because these species only overlap in a tiny part of their range, it is unlikely that many people are treated to a side-by-side comparison. Noisy flocks of either titmouse will perhaps be heard before they are seen. They forage along branches, often hanging upside-down to reach hard-to-get food items. The oak titmouse's call is a scratchy *swissy cheese!* and its song is a whistly *sweetie-sweetie-sweetie.* The juniper titmouse's call is *see-deedeedee!*

WHERE DO I FIND IT? Look for these fairly common birds foraging in small family groups, ranging across their home habitat. Oak titmice prefer oak and mixed oak-pine woodlands. This is the only titmouse found on the western side of the Sierra Nevada mountain range. Nearly all of the oak titmouse's range falls within California, with one small region of south-central Oregon being included. The juniper titmouse is found in open oak-juniper and pinyon-juniper forests of the Southwest, from Colorado and New Mexico west to California. The juniper's range barely reaches into southwestern Wyoming, southern Idaho, and Oregon. They are not found west of the Sierra Nevadas. Of the two species, the oak titmouse is more likely to be found in suburban parks and small town backyards.

WHAT CAN I FEED OR DO TO ATTRACT IT? If your backyard or neighborhood has oaks or junipers and falls within the range of one of these tiny woodland sprites, chances are a small foraging flock will visit sooner or later. Both species are eager visitors at feeding stations, where they will eat sunflower hearts, peanuts, suet, and suet dough as well as grapes and nuts. The members of the titmouse family are all cavity nesters and these two species are no exception. Both will use nest boxes for either nesting or roosting. The vast majority of nests for either oak or juniper titmice are probably placed in old woodpecker holes or excavated in rotted wood—another reason to leave dead trees or tree limbs in place where and when you can safely do so. Both species are avid visitors to backyard water features.

NESTING When a suitable cavity is found, both members of the pair work to create the nest out of soft materials like grass, plant down, moss, and bark shreds, lined with animal hair. Up to eight eggs are laid and incubated by the female for about two weeks. Young titmice fledge from the nest between two and three weeks later after being fed in the nest by both parents.

Bushtit

These are unique little birds of the western United States and Mexico. Though tiny and plain, bushtits have huge personalities, constantly on the move and usually chattering up a storm. These are highly social birds, rarely found alone. Bushtit flocks range in size from three or four birds to more than sixty, often mixing with other species, including chickadees, wrens, kinglets, and warblers. These flocks move through woodlands, brushy areas, and back-yards throughout the West in search of insect food, occasionally stopping at backyard bird feeders for seeds and suet. The bushtit is the only New World representative of the long-tailed tit family, a group of birds consisting of eleven species, most of which are found in Europe and Asia.

HOW DO I IDENTIFY IT? These tiny songbirds (about 4½ inches long) are very plain overall, sporting a brownish gray plumage with more brown in the face and belly and more gray in the back and wings. They are plump little birds with long tails and short, stubby black bills. Males and females look similar. Plumage varies geographically; Pacific Coast birds are browner overall with an obvious brown crown while inland birds are paler and grayer with a grayish crown. In all plumages, look for a small drab-colored bird with a long tail, constantly moving and foraging. Bushtits do not have a song, but they utter numerous calls, the most common of which being a soft, constant, high-pitched chip note.

WHERE DO I FIND IT? Bushtits are found year-round throughout much of the western United States, parts of eastern Texas, and Mexico. These birds do not migrate, but they may wander to nearby areas during winter. Bushtits are found in a wide variety of habitats, including forests, mountains, brushy areas, parks, and suburban backyards, though they seem to prefer oak-pine woodlands. Listen for their distinctive calls and you may be able to locate a foraging flock, perhaps in your own backyard.

WHAT CAN I FEED OR DO TO ATTRACT IT? These are not common feeder birds, but flocks of bushtits frequently pass through backyards and sometimes stop to check out a good feeding station. Their favorite feeder foods include sunflower and peanut bits, suet, and fruit pieces. Away from feeders, bushtits feed heavily on small insects, including leafhoppers, aphids, caterpillars, beetles, and ants. They also eat some berries. Planting native shrubs and small trees is usually the best way to lure bushtits into your backyard. These birds are also attracted to a good birdbath with clean, moving water. Remember to keep the water in your birdbath shallow (about 2 inches of water is ideal).

NESTING These birds build elaborate hanging nests. Males and females work together to construct the unique nests, which may take a month or more to complete. They use elastic spider web to attach the hanging nest to the branch of a shrub or tree. The nest itself is made of moss, lichens, leaves, and twigs and lined with plant down, animal fur, and feathers. The finished product is a tightly woven sac, sometimes up to a foot long, with a small entrance hole near the top. The female lays about six small, white eggs and both parents incubate them for about 12 days. Both parents feed the nestlings until they fledge after about two weeks. Bushtits typically raise two families per year.

AT A GLANCE

🏠	–
⚱	✔
🗼	✔
🌳	✔
♪	✔
🐦	–

White-breasted Nuthatch

The word "nuthatch" refers to their habit of wedging a seed in a crevice and then hacking or "hatching" it open by pounding at it with their chisel-like bill. Nuthatches are often referred to as "upside-down birds" because they forage by probing tree trunks with their heads facing downward. During their journeys down the trunk of a tree, they often pause, and then raise their head so that it is parallel to the ground—a unique posture among birds. The best-known family member is the white-breasted nuthatch, a bird of deciduous woods and tree-filled backyards. In woodlands, listen for the nuthatch's nasal honking calls anytime. Males and females always forage near each other and, in winter, in a mixed flock with chickadees and titmice.

HOW DO I IDENTIFY IT? At nearly 6 inches, the white-breasted nuthatch is the largest nuthatch. Males have gray backs with black caps, white underparts, and a beady black eye on a white face. Females are similar but wear gray on their heads. White-breasteds are thick-necked and short-tailed, with a stocky appearance. White-breasted nuthatch calls—uttered frequently in all seasons—are a nasal and repetitive *ank-ank*. If you see a medium-sized gray, black, and white bird, scooting down a tree trunk, stopping to probe with its bill, chances are you're watching a white-breasted nuthatch. Its cousins, the red-breasted of the far North and West, the brown-headed of the Southeast, and the pygmy of the western mountains, are all much smaller and less conspicuous.

WHERE DO I FIND IT? White-breasted nuthatches prefer older deciduous woods, but are found in large parks and leafy backyards. They are active birds, calling regularly and almost constantly moving, whether foraging in a natural woodland setting or at a backyard feeding station. In northern coniferous woods, and at high elevations along the Appalachian chain, they are replaced by the smaller red-breasted nuthatch, while the brown-headed nuthatch displaces them in the dry pinewoods of the South. In the West, the pygmy nuthatch occurs in pine woods of the mountains.

WHAT CAN I FEED OR DO TO ATTRACT IT? The white-breasted nuthatch eats both insects and seeds, enjoying its fare with the seasons. Insects make up nearly 100 percent of their summer diet, with seeds being added in fall and winter. Autumn's extra seeds and nuts are sometimes stashed in tree bark crevices to be eaten later. White-breasted nuthatches will come to feeders for black-oil sunflower and other seeds, peanuts, or suet, but they tend to abandon backyard feeders almost entirely in spring and summer when insects are plentiful. Nuthatches are cavity nesters, but they seem to prefer tree cavities to nest boxes. Leaving old, dead trees standing—where this can be done safely—offers nuthatches potential foraging, "hatching," and nesting sites.

NESTING Nuthatches maintain their pair bond and territory all year. The nest is placed in a natural cavity, old woodpecker hole, or, more rarely, a nest box. Built by the female, it is a cup of grasses, bark strips, and twigs lined with hair. When the nest is finished, the nuthatches "sweep" the entrance with their bills, rubbing a crushed insect against the wood—the chemicals released may repel predators. The female incubates a clutch of eight eggs for two weeks. Both parents feed the young for at least two weeks until fledging.

AT A GLANCE

🏠	✔
⛲	✔
🕯	✔
🍃	–
🎵	✔
🐦	✔

Red-breasted Nuthatch

Creeping along pine branches like a tiny mechanical toy, the red-breasted nuthatch is looking for seeds and for insects, spiders, and other edible morsels. Its small size and preference for northern coniferous forests may make it a less familiar sight to many backyard bird watchers. However, when the natural food crop is poor in the red-breasted nuthatches' year-round range in the North and the mountain areas of the East and West, these birds will venture south and to lower elevations in search of food. During these "invasion" years, red-breasted nuthatches can become familiar visitors at backyard feeding stations. Like other nuthatches, the red-breasted forages on trees by working its way from the top downward, often going all the way to the ground along the trunk before flying off to the high branches of another tree. Strong, long-toed feet with sharp claws help the nuthatch to maintain a grip on the tree bark, even when hanging upside-down.

HOW DO I IDENTIFY IT? This small nuthatch (4½ inches long) is not really red on its breast—it's more orange or rusty. Another key field mark is the bold black line through the eye, which both males and females show, though males are more richly colorful. This eyeline, the smaller size, and the male's rich rusty breast and belly help tell this nuthatch apart from the larger, more common white-breasted nuthatch. Male red-breasted nuthatches are black-headed and gray-backed, while females are gray-headed and gray-backed. The call of the red-breasted nuthatch is a series of high-pitched nasal toots, which some bird watchers say sounds like a tiny tin horn. It also gives a rapid series of toots and squeaks when excited.

WHERE DO I FIND IT? Though they will visit all kinds of trees, especially in winter, red-breasted nuthatches seem to prefer conifers of all types during most of the year, including during the breeding season. They are year-round residents in the northern forests from the Canadian Maritimes and New England to the mountain forests of the West as far as Alaska. In winter, they can be found almost anywhere in the continental United States except for the Florida peninsula and South Texas. Any large stand of pines is worth checking in winter for red-breasted nuthatches.

WHAT CAN I FEED OR DO TO ATTRACT IT? Planting conifers like pines, spruces, hemlocks, or firs will put out the welcome mat for these birds, though you may have to be patient until the trees grow large enough to produce the cones from which the nuthatches get seeds. They will also visit bird feeders, particularly for sunflower seeds and hearts, peanuts, suet, and suet dough. Their ability to cling makes it easy for them to visit any type of feeder. And it's always a good idea to have a well-maintained birdbath, since most of our backyard birds need water for drinking and bathing.

NESTING A mated pair will share the work of excavating a nesting cavity, then the female prepares the nest inside it using fine grasses, rootlets, and moss. They often spread sticky pine sap (or "pitch") around the nest cavity entrance to discourage other birds and creatures from entering. Four or more eggs are laid and incubated by the female for 12 days. The male feeds the female during incubation and both parents feed the nestlings until fledging day about three weeks later.

AT A GLANCE	
🏠	✔
🛁	✔
🔦	✔
🌿	–
🎵	✔
🐦	✔

House Wren

The rich and burbling song of the house wren is surprisingly loud for such a tiny bird (4¾ inches long). House wrens are named for their preference for living in close proximity to humans, often in tiny wren houses that we provide for them. This mostly plain brown bird makes up for its small size and drab color by being a fierce competitor for nesting sites. In fact, backyard landlords who wish to provide housing for bluebirds, swallows, and purple martins sometimes learn the hard way that it's best to place their housing away from the edge of the woods where territorial house wrens may take them over and evict the intended tenants. The house wren's song and scolding calls are heard often wherever they are present.

HOW DO I IDENTIFY IT? House wrens are notable for their lack of field marks. Their warm-brown upperparts and tail are matched by a grayish breast. Look closely at the house wren and you'll see a variety of small white and black spots, the only variation in the bird's subtly beautiful plumage. Males and females look alike and both have the habit, characteristic of wrens, of cocking their tails up when perched. The thin, slightly curved bill is ideal for capturing and eating the house wren's insect prey. As they forage in thick cover near the ground, with their small size and brown coloration, house wrens can look a lot like tiny, feathered mice.

WHERE DO I FIND IT? Spending the summers in thickets and brushy edge habitat adjacent to woodlands, the house wren is a familiar bird in parks, backyards, and gardens, often—but not always—near human settlements. They are most often heard singing their long, rich, burbling song before they are seen. Some house wrens winter in the southernmost states in the United States, but many travel beyond our borders farther south.

WHAT CAN I FEED OR DO TO ATTRACT IT? Insects and arachnids make up the house wren's diet (grasshoppers, crickets, spiders, and moths are on the menu), but they will also eat snails and caterpillars. Most of their foraging is done in thick vegetation on or near the ground. Wren houses are the best way to attract them. House wrens will readily accept nest boxes with interior dimensions of 4 × 4 inches and entry holes of 1¼ inches in diameter. Nest boxes placed adjacent to brushy habitat or a wood's edge seem to be the most attractive. Nest boxes for bluebirds and tree swallows should be placed far from edge habitat, in the open, to avoid conflict and competition from territorial house wrens.

NESTING House wrens nest in a variety of locations, from woodpecker holes to natural cavities and nest boxes. Like Carolina wrens, house wrens will also nest in flowerpots, drainpipes, and other such sites. They are very competitive about nesting sites, often filling all or most available cavities with sticks. The male builds these "dummy" nests, and the female selects one in which to nest. The twig structures are lined with soft materials, such as grass or hair, and the female lays six to eight eggs. She performs the incubation duties, which last from 12 to 14 days. Fledglings leave the nest two or more weeks after hatching. House wrens are known to pierce the eggs of other cavity-nesting birds in their territories.

AT A GLANCE	
🏠	✔
⛲	✔
🪶	–
🌿	–
♫	✔
🐦	–

Western Bluebird

The western bluebird is the common bluebird of the West. In open forests, along roadways, and on meadow fence lines these birds are a frequent sight, perching low as they watch for insects. They drop to the ground or make short flights into the air to capture their prey, returning to their hunting perch to consume it or flying off to feed it to nestlings in a nearby cavity. In winter, western bluebirds in the northern parts of their range move southward or to lower elevations, sometimes forming feeding flocks of hundreds of birds wherever their winter foods—berries and fruits—are abundant.

HOW DO I IDENTIFY IT?   A mostly blue, medium-sized songbird (7 inches long) with a blue throat, rusty breast, and blue wings and tail, the male western bluebird also has a wash of rusty color across his upper back. It is the rusty back and blue throat that help set the western bluebird apart from its cousin the eastern bluebird. Female westerns are paler version of the male, with the blue areas looking blue-gray on her. She also sports an obvious white eye ring. The call of the western bluebird is a harsh, down-slurred *tew-tew*. The song is a chattering warble that is more whistly than musical. Our other bluebird of the West is the mountain bluebird. Male mountain bluebirds are pale blue overall without any rusty color.

WHERE DO I FIND IT?   During the spring and summer breeding season, western bluebirds can be found in a variety of habitats, including open pine forests, areas that have been timbered or burned, farmland, meadows, parks, golf courses, and even our suburban backyards—anywhere there are available nesting cavities. While some western bluebirds remain as year-round residents in the Southwest and along the Pacific coast, birds from the Pacific Northwest and those nesting at higher elevations move south and may form large feeding flocks.

WHAT CAN I FEED OR DO TO ATTRACT IT?   Nest boxes placed in open habitats within the breeding range of the western bluebird are almost sure to attract their attention. You can also make sure that your landscape includes fruit- and berry-producing plants, such as juniper, elderberry, mistletoe, toyon, grape, cherry, sumac, and currant, which bluebirds eat in winter or during harsh weather. Western bluebirds will visit your feeding stations for mealworms, suet dough, and fruits such as raisins or grapes. Offer mealworms or suet bits or dough in a small dish on your deck rail, windowsill, or platform feeder. They will occasionally eat sunflower hearts at a feeder. However, they are not normally seed-eaters, so your standard seed offerings will not be to their liking. All bluebirds seem to love to bathe, so a reliable source of clean water is another excellent way to attract them.

AT A GLANCE

🏠	✔
⛲	✔
🪣	✔
🌿	✔
♪♩	✔
🐦	✔

NESTING   Bluebirds are cavity nesters, but they cannot excavate their own nesting spaces. Instead they rely on natural cavities, old woodpecker holes, or human-supplied nest boxes. The proper entry hole size for western bluebirds is 1½ inches in diameter. Males set up a territory with possible nest sites and the females choose one. She builds the interior nest from weed stems and fine grasses and deposits four to eight eggs into it. Incubation lasts about two weeks and two and a half weeks after hatching, the young bluebirds leave the nest.

Mountain Bluebird

Slightly larger than our other two North American bluebirds (7½ inches long) and pale powder blue overall, the male mountain bluebird is a subtly beautiful songbird of open spaces. As its name suggests, it nests in the mountains, in addition to many other habitats from low, treeless prairies and open ranges to sagebrush and farmland. Because it prefers open habitat, where handy sit-and-watch hunting perches are not always present, mountain bluebirds regularly hover a few feet off the ground looking for the movement of their insect prey. When trees and tree cavities are in short supply—such as in open prairie or sagebrush flats—mountain bluebirds will nest in holes in other cavities, such as holes in rocks, cliff faces, buildings, and dirt banks. They have even been known to nest in old cliff swallow nests.

HOW DO I IDENTIFY IT?   Males are light blue overall with a pale gray belly. Females are grayish on the head, breast, and belly with varying amounts of blue in their wings and tail. Mountain bluebirds appear slender, long-winged, and long-tailed when perched. By comparison, western bluebirds appear hunch-shouldered and less slender when perched. You could almost say that the mountain bluebird has better, straighter posture than the western bluebird. While the differences in blue coloration between these two bluebird species can seem easy to tell apart, they can be confusing on bright, sunny days or under cloudy skies. Remember this: if you see a bluebird with any rusty color at all, it's not a mountain bluebird. It's probably a western or eastern bluebird.

WHERE DO I FIND IT?   In summer, from central Alaska to the central Great Plains and the mountains of the Southwest, the mountain bluebird is fairly common in open pine forests, in mountain clearings, and along roadside meadows. Many bluebird organizations of the West have placed nest box trails specifically for mountain bluebirds along western roadways, giving this beautiful songbird thousands of potential nesting sites. In winter, mountain bluebirds drift to lower elevations. They frequently form large foraging flocks in winter, sometimes mixing with western bluebirds. These flocks can be found in a wide range of habitats, including desert, sagebrush, open agricultural fields, and pinyon-juniper woods.

WHAT CAN I FEED OR DO TO ATTRACT IT?   Providing nesting boxes for mountain bluebirds is a highly effective way to attract this bird to your property. It is key to make sure the entrance hole for a mountain bluebird nest box is 1⁹⁄₁₆ inches in diameter. However if you don't live in the mountain bluebird's preferred breeding habitat, you'll do better to try to attract them in winter with fruit- and berry-bearing plants, trees, shrubs, and vines. Among the bluebird-approved plant families are mistletoe, serviceberry, hackberry, and juniper. They will readily visit a water feature or birdbath—sometimes in breathtaking numbers in winter, when other water sources are frozen. They will occasionally visit bird feeders for fruits (grapes, raisins, berries) and for suet bits or dough.

AT A GLANCE	
🏠	✔
⛲	✔
🗼	✔
🌿	✔
🎵	✔
🐦	✔

NESTING   Once they find a suitable cavity for nesting, both adults build a nest inside from grasses, rootlets, and pine needles, lined with softer materials. The female lays five to eight eggs and incubates them for at least two weeks. Both parents feed the nestlings for three weeks before they fledge and for almost a month afterwards.

American Robin

You don't need to be a bird watcher to know the American robin. Who hasn't seen one of these birds running along a lawn, pausing every so often to stare down an unlucky earthworm? The robin's familiar cheerily-cheerio *song meshes well with the thunk of basketballs and the drone of lawnmowers in suburban neighborhoods all across North America. You may be surprised to learn that American robins aren't robins at all—they are actually thrushes. What happened is this: When English settlers first visited the New World, they saw these red-breasted birds everywhere and were reminded of the similarly colored European robins from back home. So they started calling these new birds "robins" too. The name stuck. Many people consider robins to be a sign of spring, but the truth is that many robins stay in their home range*

year-round. They just tend to go unnoticed since they spend most of the winter months in woodlands looking for berries. As soon as the weather starts warming up again, the local robins reappear on lawns everywhere.

HOW DO I IDENTIFY IT? These are fairly large, chunky songbirds that are dark grayish overall with red-orange underneath. Adult males sport brick-red breasts and black heads with a streaked white throat and lower belly. Females are paler overall. Young robins have heavy spots on the breast for their first few months out of the nest. Robins are very vocal birds, often the first to sing in the wee hours of the morning and the last to quiet down at night. Listen for their *puk-puk-puk* calls year-round.

WHERE DO I FIND IT? You don't need to look far. The robin is basically a bird of lawns with trees and shrubs, though it also breeds in high mountain forests near clear-cuts or openings. Few other species show its adaptability to diverse habitats, from landscaped parking lot islets to dense, secluded forests. In winter, look for these birds in woodlands where berries are plentiful.

WHAT CAN I FEED OR DO TO ATTRACT IT? By mowing the lawn regularly and planting dense evergreens and fruit-bearing shrubs and trees, we unintentionally provide perfect conditions for robins. This is one reason why these birds are so plentiful throughout much of their range. They seldom visit feeders but will eat bread, chopped raisins, grapes, and crumbled, moistened dog chow in severe winter weather. Robins gather in large flocks in fall and winter to raid fruiting trees and shrubs, fluttering and giggling as they reach for food. They are especially attracted to crabapples, Virginia creeper, honeysuckle, and wild strawberry plants.

NESTING You may be familiar with the robin's sturdy mud-and-grass cup, often nestled in an evergreen, a climbing vine, on a horizontal branch, or even on a windowsill or porch light. The female incubates three to four bluish eggs for about two weeks. Adults can be seen running around with bills full of earthworms as soon as the young hatch. The young leave the nest, barely able to flutter, on about the thirteenth day. You can recognize them by their spotted, whitish breasts and reedy, begging calls. The male feeds them for another three weeks, while the female usually starts a second family. By planting junipers and spruces, you can provide year-round shelter for robins and also increase the chances of them nesting in your yard.

AT A GLANCE	
🏠	✔
⛲	✔
🪶	–
🍇	✔
🎵	✔
🐦	✔

European Starling

In 1889, there were no European starlings in North America, yet today—just over a century later—we have more than two hundred million. Blame a fan of William Shakespeare. In 1890, a flock of a hundred starlings was released in New York's Central Park in an attempt to bring to America all the bird species mentioned in Shakespeare's plays. The adaptable starling soon spread westward in one of history's greatest avian population explosions. You are not likely to ever encounter a quiet starling—these birds are incredibly vocal, displaying an astonishing ability to mimic other bird songs, sirens, voices, barks, or mechanical sounds. They do this year-round and can be very convincing at times. In fact, if you think you may be hearing the song of a meadowlark or some other bird during the dead of winter when most songbirds are not singing, look around for a talented starling instead.

HOW DO I IDENTIFY IT? These medium-sized birds (8½ inches long) are glossy black overall with a bright yellow bill during spring and summer. Up close, you can see the green and purple in the starling's iridescent plumage. In winter, starlings are duller overall, covered with white spots (little stars, or "starlings") with a blackish bill. Starlings are almost always found in flocks. In flight, they flap their triangular-shaped wings rapidly.

WHERE DO I FIND IT? Most Americans can see a starling simply by looking out their window. These birds cover the entire North American continent year-round, except for the far North in winter. Starlings can be found in just about every habitat type, though they are most common in areas where humans are present, such as farms, cities, and suburbs. They are least common in remote, pristine habitats. In fall, starlings form gigantic, noisy flocks roaming in search of food and roosting sites. These flocks can be made up of hundreds of thousands of birds.

WHAT CAN I FEED OR DO TO ATTRACT IT? Many bird watchers consider starlings a pest at their feeders and birdhouses. To discourage starlings at your feeder, simply remove the foods they prefer: suet, peanuts, bread, and cracked corn. (If, instead, you'd like to attract more starlings to your backyard, simply do the opposite!) When not visiting feeders, starlings keep a regular diet of insects, berries, fruits, and seeds, but they are not picky eaters—they're just as willing to eat French fries from a dumpster as they are to find bugs on our lawns or suet at our feeders. The starling's traditional foraging technique is to insert its long, sharp bill into the ground and then open it to expose beetle grubs and other prey.

NESTING Starlings are cavity nesters that cannot excavate their own holes, so they use existing cavities, such as woodpecker holes, pipes, crevices in buildings, and birdhouses. Sites are often stolen from other, less aggressive cavity nesters, such as bluebirds or purple martins. (To exclude starlings from your nest boxes, make sure the entry holes are 1⁹⁄₁₆ inches or less in diameter.) Once a male has a site, a female will help finish the nest—a messy affair of grass, feathers, paper, and plastic. Between four to six eggs are laid and incubated by both parents for about 12 days. Young starlings leave the nest three weeks later.

AT A GLANCE	
🏠	✔
(bird bath)	✔
(feeder)	✔
(plant)	–
♫	✔
(birds)	–

Cedar Waxwing

A beady, insect-like trill first alerts many bird watchers to the presence of cedar waxwings, as they tend to completely blend into the surrounding foliage. These wandering fruit-eaters appear and disappear seemingly without rhyme or reason, descending to strip a tree of its fruits and then whirling off to parts unknown. Fermented fruits sometimes cause entire flocks of waxwings to stagger about on the ground until their intoxication wears off. Cedar waxwings travel in tight flocks to locate and feed on small fruits. They may be completely hidden in leaves as they flutter and pluck fruit, only to explode out with reedy calls and a rush of wings when startled. In late summer, they may be seen in twisting, dodging pursuits of winged insects over water. Waxwings get their name from the red secretions on the tips of their wing feathers, which look like shiny drops of sealing wax. Worldwide, there are only two other species of waxwing: the Bohemian and Japanese waxwings. Waxwings are related to silky flycatchers, a largely tropical family of birds.

HOW DO I IDENTIFY IT?   Overall, these birds are medium-sized (about 7 inches long), dressed in a warm, brownish gray plumage, and have crests like cardinals and blue jays. "Sleek" is the word most often used to describe the silky fawn plumage of the cedar waxwing. A velvety black bandit mask hides the eyes, and a bright yellow band tips the gray tail. You may occasionally encounter a cedar waxwing with orange rather than yellow tail tips. This is caused by the bird's diet. When a young, developing waxwing eats the red fruit of certain honeysuckle species, it grows orange tail feathers.

WHERE DO I FIND IT?   The cedar waxwing's only real habitat requirement is the presence of fruit-bearing trees and shrubs, so it can be found everywhere except grasslands, deserts, and deep interior forests. Thought to be nomadic, the species does make a poorly understood migration that takes it as far south as southern Central America. Cedar waxwings are most often seen in flocks in fall and winter.

WHAT CAN I FEED OR DO TO ATTRACT IT?   These birds are not likely to visit your bird feeders. Attracting cedar waxwings is best accomplished by planting the trees and shrubs they prefer—serviceberry, hawthorn, firethorn, dogwood, chokecherry, viburnum, native honeysuckle, blueberry, cedar, and others that bear small fruits. They may also visit birdbaths, especially those with moving water.

NESTING   While many bird species are strongly territorial, cedar waxwings do not defend a territory at all. In fact, they are sometimes semi-colonial, nesting close together with other waxwing neighbors. However, these birds are monogamous. Both sexes help build a bulky, cup-shaped nest in the outer canopy of a tree. Leaves, straw, twigs, and string are used to construct the nest. Sometimes waxwings gather these materials by stealing from other birds' nests. The female lays four eggs and incubates them for 12 days, while the male feeds her. Young are fed on insects for the first two days, then solely on regurgitated fruits, leaving the nest around 15 days later. This fruit-based diet ensures that any parasitic brown-headed cowbirds hatching in their nests do not survive. Large flocks of immature birds (identifiable by their yellowish, streaked bellies) linger near breeding grounds for one or two months after the adults leave.

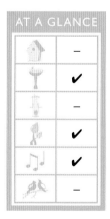

AT A GLANCE

	–
	✔
	–
	✔
	✔
	–

Yellow-rumped Warbler

Warblers are some of the coolest birds around. Ask a bird watcher what it was that got them hooked on birding, and many of them will probably mention going on a bird walk in April and May during the peak of spring migration and being overwhelmed by the sheer beauty and diversity of this interesting group of birds. Most warblers are colorful, great singers, and highly migratory. Because of their migratory nature and because they are mostly insect-eaters, warblers are not often thought of as backyard birds. Most people hit the local park or find a good nature trail to see warblers. However, many of these birds do pass through North American backyards during spring and fall, often completely unnoticed. One of the most widespread and numerous of these warblers—and the most likely one to encounter in your backyard—is the yel-low-rumped warbler, a.k.a. "butterbutt." Yellow-rumped warblers found in western states look a little different from their eastern counterparts—in fact, they used to be considered two separate species.

HOW DO I IDENTIFY IT?   Butterbutts are 5 to 6 inches long, with a sharp thin bill and slightly notched tail. In spring and summer, the male is blue-gray with either a white (eastern birds) or yellow (western birds) throat and white belly, black streaking on its back, a black face patch, two white wing bars, black bib, and yellow spots on the crown, shoulders, and rump. Spring females are browner and duller than their mates. Immatures and fall adults are brown above, with brown-streaked underparts and little or no yellow visible. Despite that long list of markings and plumage variations, there's really just one thing you need to look for: the bright yellow rump. That, along with a frequent and distinctive *check!* note, will quickly identify these birds year-round.

WHERE DO I FIND IT?   These birds breed in the far North and throughout much of the western United States. In the East, they are known only as a migrant or winter resident. Migrants can be found in backyards, woodlands, hedgerows, thickets, and even along beaches as they stream through in large flocks. Winter birds congregate wherever they can find berries, their primary cold-weather food. Yellow-rumped warblers can be found year-round in parts of the West.

WHAT CAN I FEED OR DO TO ATTRACT IT?   Though not common feeder birds, yellow-rumped warblers will sometimes visit bird feeders for sunflower seed bits, suet or suet dough, raisins, and fruits. They've also been known to raid hummingbird feeders for sugar water. The best way to attract these birds is by providing natural food via fruit-producing plants—bayberries and junipers are their favorites. Yellow-rumps also readily visit backyard water features for drinking and bathing.

NESTING   For nesting, the yellow-rumped warbler selects conifer forests, generally spruce, pine, or cedar. The female builds the nest on a horizontal branch, anywhere from 5 to 50 feet high in the tree, using bark, twigs, weeds, and roots to create an open cup that is then lined with hair and feathers. The female incubates the four or five eggs for 12 to 13 days. When the chicks hatch, both parents feed them for 10 to 12 days until fledging, and then the male feeds them for a time afterward. There are usually two broods per year.

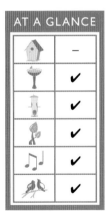

AT A GLANCE	
🏠	—
🛁	✔
🪶	✔
🌿	✔
🎵	✔
🐦	✔

Spotted Towhee

If you look in a bird book published before 1995, you won't find the spotted towhee. Prior to that, the spotted towhee, a widespread and common bird of the West, was considered to be a western type of the rufous-sided towhee. After that we had two towhees with rufous sides: the spotted towhee (named for the large white spots on its black wings) and the eastern towhee. The name "towhee" comes from the call that these species make, which sounds like tow-hee! *or* chee-wink! *Towhees are actually large, ground-loving sparrows. They are nearly always found on or near the ground when foraging and even frequently nest on the ground. The exception may be during the spring courtship, when males sometimes sing from an exposed, elevated perch when trying to attract a mate.*

HOW DO I IDENTIFY IT?   A black hood around a bright red eye, bright white spots on a black back and wings, rufous sides, a pale belly, and a long black tail edged in white describes the male spotted towhee. Females are chocolate-brown on the head, back, wings, and tail where the males are black. Towhees have a large, dark bill. They are large birds (8 inches), looking much bigger and longer-tailed than most of their relatives in the sparrow family. The song of the spotted towhee is *chup-chup-chup-zreeee!* and its regular call is a rising, mewing *zreeee!*

WHERE DO I FIND IT?   Spotted towhees love a messy, brushy habitat. From the Central Great Plains west to southern British Columbia and south to Mexico, the spotted towhee is a common bird in chaparral, mesquite thickets, scrub habitats, and open woods with some brushy tangles. In particularly dense habitat, you might hear them calling or scratching on the ground before you spot them. They use their large feet to scratch aside leaf litter and ground cover, hoping to expose beetles, caterpillars, spiders, ants, and other goodies. Spotted towhees in arid portions of the West and along the Pacific coast are year-round residents. Birds that nest in the western Great Plains move south in winter. They are also common in winter on the southern Great Plains.

WHAT CAN I FEED OR DO TO ATTRACT IT?   If your property has an area of messy undergrowth or shrubby thickets, you've got prime spotted towhee habitat. If you do not have such habitat naturally, you can always use fallen or trimmed tree branches to create a brush pile, which towhees and many other birds will happily use. Towhees can be shy about coming very far out into the open. Since they love to scratch through leaf litter to find food, it's a good idea to let leaves and other natural ground cover accumulate. Mixed seed, cracked corn, millet, milo, and sunflower seeds scattered on the ground (or on a low platform feeder), especially near thick cover, will attract spotted towhees. Birdbaths with moving water are highly appealing to spotted towhees, too.

NESTING   Spotted towhees nest on or near the ground in a well-concealed spot, where the female builds a nest woven out of grass, rootlets, small twigs, and dried leaves. She lays three to six eggs and incubates them for about 12 days. Young towhees remain in the nest for about 10 days after hatching, during which time both parents share the feeding chores.

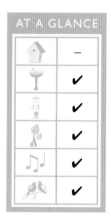

AT A GLANCE	
🏠	—
⛲	✔
🕯	✔
🌾	✔
🎵	✔
🐦	✔

Chipping Sparrow

A close look at these natty little birds reveals much to admire in its quiet and confiding ways. As common as they are around backyards and parks, we know surprisingly little about the chipping sparrow's mating habits. One Ontario study showed males not to be monogamous, as assumed, but to mate freely. These birds have the interesting habit of lining their nests with animal hair. They'll also use human hair, but more on that later.

HOW DO I IDENTIFY IT? A rusty beret and bold, white eyeline are the best field marks of this slender little sparrow. Plain gray underparts, a streaked brown back, and a small, all-black bill set off its striking head markings. The chipping sparrow is one of our smallest sparrows (about 5½ inches long). It is an underappreciated bird, perhaps because it is so small and unobtrusive. Listen for its rather dry, monotonous trills (sometimes compared to the sound of a sewing machine) as well as its signature chipping notes.

WHERE DO I FIND IT? In summer, these birds are found throughout Canada and much of the United States. They can be found year-round in the southeastern United States. Before the massive expansion of suburbs, chipping sparrows were limited to open, grassy coniferous forests and parklike woodlands with shrubby understories. Our suburban habitats have just the right mix of short grass, shrubbery, and conifers that chipping sparrows need, so we can enjoy their company on our doorsteps and sidewalks. Although northern populations are strongly migratory, southern birds flock up but tend to stay near their breeding grounds. Winter flocks of up to fifty birds perch in trees, descending en masse to the ground to peck for seeds and then adjourning to treetops before the next feeding bout.

WHAT CAN I FEED OR DO TO ATTRACT IT? Chipping sparrows forage primarily on or near the ground, feasting on weed and grass seeds and some smaller fruits. They're easy to please at backyard feeding stations, with black-oil sunflower seeds and cracked corn being among their favorite feeder foods. Chipping sparrows also love mixed seeds, suet, rolled oats, and mealworms. They'll come to hopper-style feeders or feed directly on the ground. Bird feeders aren't the only way to cater to backyard chipping sparrows. These birds also greatly appreciate baked and crushed eggshells strewn on a sidewalk. But it's most fun to offer them human or pet hair clippings. A trip to any salon can net a season's worth, and you may have the pleasure of finding a used nest lined with your own hair—the ultimate vanity piece for the discerning homeowner.

NESTING Planting shrubs and vines—such as creepers and honeysuckles—can increase the chances of these birds nesting in your yard. Female chipping sparrows weave lovely little nests of thin twigs and weed stems, with a center composed of animal hair. These are often concealed in low trees and shrubs, but are easily located by the shrilling of older nestlings. Females incubate the four eggs for around 12 days, and the young leave the nest about 9 to 12 days later. Chipping sparrows feed insects to their young, sometimes flycatching on the wing. Streaky, brown, and nondescript, the young are fed by their parents for three more weeks before forming juvenile flocks.

AT A GLANCE	
🏠	—
🏺	✔
💧	✔
🌿	✔
🎵	✔
🐦	—

American Tree Sparrow

You're most likely to encounter American tree sparrows during the winter months, when they abandon their summer home in the Arctic and migrate into southern Canada and the northern two-thirds of the United States. In winter, these birds become quite common in open fields, brushy areas, and just about any backyard with a well-stocked feeding station. The "tree" part of this bird's name is misleading—woodlands and forests are some of the last places you're likely to find an American tree sparrow. In fact, these birds nest in the northernmost areas of the Arctic tundra, where there are few trees at all. They were named by early European settlers who were reminded of the Eurasian tree sparrow of the Old World (there is a superficial resemblance between the two species). As the saying goes, the rest was history.

HOW DO I IDENTIFY IT? The American tree sparrow is a small gray bird (5½ inches long) with a bright rufous crown and an obvious black splotch on the center of an otherwise unmarked breast. The bird's cone-shaped bill is conspicuously two-toned, with dark above and yellow below. The back and wings are handsomely marked with rust, gray, and white. Because songbirds generally sing only on their breeding grounds, and American tree sparrows breed in the Arctic, you're not likely to hear the male's sweet, whistling song in your backyard. But you may hear the soft call notes given between tree sparrows in a foraging winter flock.

WHERE DO I FIND IT? Don't look for these birds in areas with lots of trees. You're much better off looking in old, brushy fields with a good supply of weeds (these birds feed heavily on weed seeds). American tree sparrows are found in flocks ranging from only a dozen to more than two hundred birds. Look along the ground near brushy areas and listen for the birds' soft call notes. When flushed from the ground, they tend to fly up and perch in a nearby tree, where they are easy to spot. Perhaps the best place to look for American tree sparrows is at a bird feeder—in many areas, these are very common winter feeder birds.

WHAT CAN I FEED OR DO TO ATTRACT IT? From late fall to early spring, American tree sparrows flock to backyard bird feeders throughout southern Canada and much of the United States. They are most attracted to white proso millet, which is found in most good seed mixes. They may also eat sunflower chips, cracked corn, and suet. American tree sparrows are ground feeders, so offer seed either directly on the ground or on a platform feeder. Away from the feeding station, these birds feed heavily on weed seeds, so a yard with dandelions, goldenrods, coneflowers, and various grasses is likely to attract decent numbers of tree sparrows.

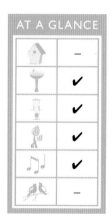

AT A GLANCE

(birdhouse)	–
(feeder)	✔
(birdbath)	✔
(perch)	✔
(song notes)	✔
(birds)	–

NESTING Back home in the northernmost regions of the continent, American tree sparrows construct nests of grasses, twigs, and moss on or near the ground. Females incubate three to five brownish eggs for about 12 days, and the young leave the nest when they're about 8 days old. After a few more days, the young tree sparrows are able to fly but are still fed by the parents for about two more weeks before gaining full independence.

Song Sparrow

These are among the most common birds in North America. Most brownish striped sparrows you see are going to be song sparrows. Look for them in a variety of habitats, from brushy fields to woodland edges to suburban back-yards. True to its name, song sparrows sing often, sometimes year-round. If there's a resident song sparrow in your yard, you'll probably hear is cheery notes at first light—as reliable as, but more pleasant than, a rooster's. One of the best-studied birds in North America, the song sparrow was the subject of Margaret Morse Nice's groundbreaking behavioral study in the 1930s. Much of what scientists understand about how songbirds choose and defend territories began with this study.

HOW DO I IDENTIFY IT? The plumage of song sparrows varies widely throughout the continent, but always look for a smallish brown and gray streaky sparrow (6 inches long) with a long tail. Their white breasts are heavily streaked and marked with a messy central spot. A grayish, striped face and crown and warm-brown upperparts complete the description. Flight is low and jerky, with the tail twisting distinctively. Three introductory notes leading to a variable jumble of trills and chips distinguish its song. Males and females look similar.

WHERE DO I FIND IT? Though song sparrows occupy a wide range of habitats, they are most often found in shrubbery near water, from small streams to beach habitats. Often you will find them walking along the water's edge like a sandpiper. Song sparrows tend to be migratory in northern areas and year-round residents in the southern United States; this varies by population. The song sparrow is one of the most variable songbirds known. Birds in the Pacific Northwest, for example, are larger, darker, and heavier-billed compared to Southeastern coastal song sparrows. There may be as many as thirty different types of song sparrows in North America.

WHAT CAN I FEED OR DO TO ATTRACT IT? Song sparrows readily visit bird feeders for sunflower seeds, cracked corn, and mixed seeds. They'll spend a lot of time on the ground under your feeders, looking for dropped seeds. Peanut butter–based suet mixes are a favorite food, and song sparrows will appear to beg at windows for such tasty fare. The song sparrow's diet varies seasonally, with insects being its primary prey in spring and summer and with seeds and fruits dominating in fall and winter. Most of the song sparrow's foraging takes place on the ground, where it will scratch and kick about in leaf litter and grasses for weed seeds and insects.

NESTING The persistent singing of song sparrows is linked to strong territorial behavior; where they are resident year-round, they tend to defend territories year-round. Territory boundaries are quite stable from year to year. Both sexes defend their territory, and they tend to stay with one mate. Females construct a bulky nest of bark strips and weed and grass stems, well hidden deep in a dense shrub. Small, ornamental evergreens are irresistible to song sparrows. The female incubates three to five eggs for about 13 days. Young birds leave the nest at only 10 days and may be fed by the parents for the next 20 days before they are fully independent. They are fond of water and will often nest near a water garden or backyard pond.

AT A GLANCE	
🏠	—
(bird bath)	✔
(feeder)	✔
(plant)	✔
♪	✔
(birds)	—

White-throated Sparrow

Old Sam Peabody, Peabody, Peabody *is the sweet whistled song of the white-throated sparrow. In Canada, where this species spends the breeding season, the song is transcribed as* Oh sweet Canada, Canada, Canada—*but there's no arguing that the white-throated sparrow's song is easy to recognize and one of the most interesting musical sounds of the avian world. From September to March these northern breeders occupy the eastern United States, in loose flocks with other sparrows, brightening winter days with their cheery sounds. Look for white-throated sparrows on the ground beneath your feeders from late fall through early spring. If your feeders are some distance from cover, consider moving them closer to the woods' edge or adding a brush pile nearby to make woodland birds (such as white-throated sparrows) feel more at home.*

HOW DO I IDENTIFY IT? The first field mark most people notice on the white-throated sparrow is not the white throat but the black-and-white striped head pattern with a yellow spot between the eyes and bill. Even at a distance this striking pattern is obvious. Some white-throated sparrows have tan-striped heads and a tannish throat. These belong to the tan-striped variety of the species (though at one time, the common belief was that these were young birds not yet in adult plumage). This medium-sized sparrow (6¾ inches long) has a gray breast and a brown, lightly patterned back.

WHERE DO I FIND IT? Spending most of the summer in the coniferous forests of the far north and New England, white-throated sparrows spend fall and winter far to the south, where they are regulars at bird feeders and in brushy edge habitats. They can be found in the New England states year-round. They prefer a habitat with thick underbrush and are found near the edge of the woods, along hedgerows, and in brushy thickets in parks and backyards. Listen for their loud, sharp *chink* calls as they move about in winter flocks, often hidden from view.

WHAT CAN I FEED OR DO TO ATTRACT IT? White-throated sparrows prefer to feed on the ground. In spring and summer, the white-throated sparrow's diet is focused on insects and arachnids—ants, grubs, and spiders—that it uncovers as it scratches through the leaf litter, much like a towhee does. In fall, the diet shifts to include berries; in winter, it includes mostly seeds from grasses. At bird feeders white-throated sparrows are attracted to mixed seed, cracked corn, and sunflower or peanut bits. But their real favorite is white proso millet—that small, round, cream-colored seed found in most basic seed mixes. (You can also buy white millet by itself from many seed suppliers.) Try offering seed on a platform feeder or directly on the ground to make your feeding station especially accommodating for these birds.

NESTING White-throated sparrows nest on or near the ground in a well-concealed spot. The cup-shaped nest is built by the female from grass, pine needles, and twigs and lined with soft material, such as rootlets or fur. The female incubates the four to five eggs for about two weeks; the male assists her in feeding the nestlings for the nine days prior to fledging. The young birds rely on the parents for food for about another two weeks.

AT A GLANCE	
🏠	–
🏺	✔
🪣	✔
🌱	✔
🎵	✔
🐦	–

Dark-eyed Junco

Most Americans are familiar with the dark-eyed junco. Even those who don't watch birds often have probably noticed these common gray-and-white birds in their backyards. Dark-eyed juncos are often called "snowbirds" because they seem to show up at our feeders and in our backyards at the same time as the first snows begin falling over much of the country. For many of us, winter is the only time we have dark-eyed juncos around. They form large flocks in backyards, parks and pastures and along rural roadsides and woodland edges in just about every corner of the United States except southern Florida. Watch for the flash of white from their tail feathers as they dart between brush piles or scatter from feeding on the ground beneath a bird feeder.

HOW DO I IDENTIFY IT?   Juncos are medium-sized sparrows (6¼ inches long), but unlike most sparrows, their plumage lacks streaking. Dark gray above and white below (or "gray skies above, snow below"), the junco has a cone-shaped, pinkish bill and flashes its white outer tail feathers in flight. Male juncos in the East are a darker gray than the overall brownish-colored females. Western juncos show a variety of plumage colors, and many of these color forms were considered separate species until recently. Now they are all lumped into a single species: dark-eyed junco. Juncos make a variety of sounds, all of them high-pitched tinkling trills, especially when flushed from cover. Their songs are very similar to those of the chipping sparrow—sometimes it's difficult to tell the two species apart when you can't see the singer.

WHERE DO I FIND IT?   These birds can be found throughout most of North America at some point in the year. In winter, they can be found in every state. Look for them in brushy areas, fields, and, of course, your backyard. They are often seen scratching through leaf litter, grass, or snow when looking for food. In spring, most juncos retreat to the far-north woods of Canada to breed, though the New England states and some areas in the West have juncos year-round. Spring migration begins as early as March and continues through early June. Fall migration occurs from mid-August through October.

WHAT CAN I FEED OR DO TO ATTRACT IT?   Juncos find their food on the ground, so in backyards they tend to hang around beneath bird feeders, picking through dropped seeds. They love white millet, which is found in most mixed wild birdseed blends and can also be purchased separately. Place some millet on a platform feeder or directly on the ground for best results. Another effective way to attract juncos is by building a brush pile near your feeding station. In spring and summer, juncos shift their diet from seeds to mostly insects, including caterpillars, grasshoppers, and spiders, and berries.

NESTING   The junco's nest is a simple, open cup of grasses and leaves, loosely woven and lined with finer grasses, fur, or feathers. Nests are normally located on the ground in a concealed spot and built by the female. She incubates her three to five eggs for almost two weeks; the male helps with feeding chores once the young hatch. Within two weeks the young birds leave the nest, and the parents are free to start another brood if the season permits.

AT A GLANCE	
🏠	—
🛁	✔
🪔	✔
🌿	✔
🎵	✔
🐦	✔

Black-headed Grosbeak

Black-headed grosbeaks are familiar summer birds of western deciduous woodlands and a welcome visitor to any backyard, where they may stay and nest if there is adequate food and shelter available. The black-headed grosbeak is closely related to the rose-breasted grosbeak of the East, and the two species sometimes interbreed where their ranges overlap in the central United States. Grosbeaks possess massive bills that allow them not only to crack open large seeds but also to crush large insects and snails. Black-headed grosbeaks are year-round residents in parts of Mexico, where they frequently prey on monarch butterflies. Monarch butterflies are toxic to most birds, but the black-headed grosbeak is one of the few bird species that is able to eat them.

HOW DO I IDENTIFY IT? These are medium-sized songbirds (about 8 inches long) with gigantic cone-shaped bills. During spring and summer, adult males are black and orange overall with mostly black heads, burnt orange bodies, and black-and-white wings. Their tails are black. Females are brownish overall with brown and white streaks on the back and wings and buffy orange underparts. Both males and females sing a whistled warble that resembles the song of an American robin, only more hurried and sweeter overall. Also listen for their loud call notes, a sharp *pik!*

WHERE DO I FIND IT? Black-headed grosbeaks spend their summers across western North America and migrate south to Mexico during winter. Their preferred habitats include deciduous woodlands and mountainous areas, though during spring and fall migration they can show up just about anywhere, including any type of open woodland or woodland edge, brushy areas, along streams, and even backyards. Look up, towards the tops of large trees where these birds tend to forage, and listen for their *pik* call notes.

WHAT CAN I FEED OR DO TO ATTRACT IT? Overall, black-headed grosbeaks keep a varied diet of insects, berries, and seeds. This gives backyard bird watchers several options for attracting them. First, try offering black-oil or striped sunflower seeds in a hopper-style feeder. These popular feeders resemble small barns or gazebos and have lots of elbow room, which is great for larger birds like grosbeaks. You can also offer safflower seeds, cracked corn, or even fruit pieces. Black-headed grosbeaks frequently drink sugar water from hummingbird or oriole feeders. Second, you can try attracting grosbeaks by planting fruit-bearing vines, shrubs, and trees. Some good options include honeysuckle, mistletoe, and juniper; they also eat poison ivy and poison oak, which you can leave if you like. These birds will also visit a good birdbath with moving water for drinking and bathing.

NESTING Black-headed grosbeaks may nest in your backyard if there is sufficient cover (large shrubs and trees) and a reliable food source. The female builds a bulky nest of twigs, weeds, rootlets, and pine needles, usually lined with plant fibers and animal hair. She lays three or four eggs, which are pale blue and splotched with reddish brown. Both parents incubate the eggs for about two weeks and then feed the nestlings for about 12 days until fledging occurs. When the young leave the nest, they are unable to fly and continue to be fed by the parents for an additional two weeks before achieving full independence. Black-headed grosbeaks typically raise only one family per year.

AT A GLANCE	
🏠	—
🛁	✔
🌾	✔
🌱	✔
🎵	✔
🐦	✔

Red-winged Blackbird

For some folks, it just isn't summer without a male red-winged blackbird's loud conk-a-ree *song coming from a nearby field or marsh. Red-winged blackbirds are true harbingers of spring in many areas. The red-winged blackbird's name succinctly describes the male's handsome plumage, yet the females of this ubiquitous species have baffled many an observer. Their streaky brown plumage is confusingly sparrowlike. Studies have shown that one dominant male red-winged blackbird may have many adult females nesting in his territory. Red-winged blackbirds are present continent-wide for most of the year. Wet meadows, swamps, and salt marshes are common habitats for these birds, especially in spring and summer.*

HOW DO I IDENTIFY IT?   The *conk-a-ree* call of the male red-winged blackbird fills the air over marshes and fields all across North America. As he gives this call, announcing himself loudly to rivals and potential mates alike, he spreads his shoulders *just so,* showing bright red and yellow shoulder patches against his black wings. During winter, some people don't recognize these birds as red-winged blackbirds because the males aren't showing off those bright red wing patches. Redwings are medium-sized blackbirds (8¾ inches long) with an all-black body, an orange-red and yellow patch on the shoulder, and a nearly conical black bill. Females are streaky brown overall, but their longer bill helps distinguish them from the sparrows (which have stouter bills).

WHERE DO I FIND IT?   Look for these common blackbirds perched on telephone wires or cattails. Wet meadows, cattail marshes, upland grasslands, and pastures are all prime breeding habitat for red-winged blackbirds. In fall and winter, they may join with other blackbird species to form huge flocks. Northern nesting redwings migrate (starting in September and October) to the southern United States, while southern nesting birds are nonmigratory. Fall blackbird flocks move during the day in oblong, loose clouds of birds. These flocks forage by day in agricultural fields and are often persecuted as a nuisance species for the crop damage they inflict. Spring migration begins in mid-February and continues through mid-May.

WHAT CAN I FEED OR DO TO ATTRACT IT?   If you live on a farm or near any open fields or marshes, you have an excellent chance of attracting red-winged blackbirds to your feeders. The red-winged blackbird's diet is mostly plant matter—weed seeds, grain, sunflower seeds, and tree seeds—along with some insects, all of which are gleaned from the ground. They will also visit feeding stations for sunflower seeds, cracked corn, peanuts, and suet. These birds are most likely to visit feeders during harsh winter weather. Surprisingly, they are able to use a variety of feeder types. Red-winged blackbirds also relish the seeds from certain vines, such as trumpet vines.

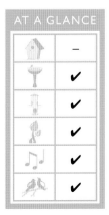

AT A GLANCE	
🏠	–
🛁	✔
🗼	✔
🌾	✔
🎵	✔
🐦	✔

NESTING   Nesting starts early for the red-winged blackbird, with males singing from an exposed perch in their territories as early as February in the South, later in the North. Females choose a nest site in a male's territory and build cup-shaped grass nests that are suspended from vertical supporting vegetation. Mud forms the foundation of the nest and soft grasses are the inner lining. Clutch size is three to four eggs, and the female alone incubates them for 10 to 13 days. Both parents care for the nestlings for about two weeks, until they are ready to leave the nest.

Brewer's Blackbird

The Brewer's blackbird is the most common and widespread blackbird of the West. At first, you may be tempted to write this species off as "just a black-bird," but a closer look reveals a beautiful mix of blues, greens, and purples on the breeding male, all of which are set off by a striking yellow eye. These brilliant colors have earned the Brewer's blackbird several interesting nick-names, including "Satin Bird" and "Glossy Blackbird." Brewer's blackbirds are commonly encountered in residential areas, where they frequently visit bird feeders for cracked corn and other offerings. You can also find these birds in plowed fields, meadows, parking lots, and parks, and even along beaches. Like other blackbirds, this species is often found in large flocks, especially during winter. Listen for their constant chuck *calls.*

HOW DO I IDENTIFY IT? These are medium-sized birds (9 inches long) with long tails and thin, pointed bills. Spring and summer males appear glossy black overall. Depending on the lighting, you may see purple, blue, and green iridescence on Brewer's blackbirds. Females and winter males are drab brown overall. Males have bright yellow eyes year-round, which help separate this species from other blackbirds. Females have dark eyes. The great-tailed grackle is another common blackbird of the West whose plumage resembles the Brewer's blackbird, but keep in mind that the grackle is much larger than the Brewer's. Great-tailed grackles are almost crow-sized; the Brewer's blackbird is robin-sized. Both males and females "sing" a short, unmusical *kwee!*

WHERE DO I FIND IT? Brewer's blackbirds can be found just about anywhere in the West, from urban parking lots to rural farm fields. Almost any open habitat is likely to have some of these birds. Brewer's blackbirds are resident in the westernmost part of their range from Washington south to the Mexican border and east to Utah. They breed throughout western Canada and the upper Midwest and winter throughout the southern United States, though they are most common in the western portions of these areas. In spring and fall, migrating birds can be found throughout the central United States, east to Ohio.

WHAT CAN I FEED OR DO TO ATTRACT IT? Blackbirds love cracked corn. Offer cracked corn either on a platform feeder or directly on the ground and you should have a decent number of Brewer's blackbirds in no time. These birds are also attracted to suet, peanut bits, and seed mixes, particularly those containing milo. Away from the feeders, Brewer's blackbirds eat a lot of insects, which they find by walking along wet fields, farmlands, and suburban lawns. They also feed heavily on weed seeds. You can entice these birds into your yard by allowing certain weeds to remain, such as knotweeds, which contain seeds that are relished by many bird species, including pheasants, quails, doves, juncos, finches, sparrows, and, of course, blackbirds. Brewer's blackbirds also love a good birdbath, especially one with moving water.

NESTING These birds often nest in colonies of up to one hundred pairs in open areas throughout the West, usually near water. Females build the nests, typically in a tree but sometimes on the ground, using a variety of twigs, grasses, weeds, and animal hair. Three to seven pale gray eggs are incubated for about two weeks. Both parents feed the young until they fledge, typically two weeks after hatching.

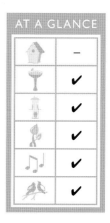

AT A GLANCE	
🏠	–
⛲	✔
🪶	✔
🌾	✔
♪	✔
🐦	✔

Common Grackle

Grackles are large, conspicuous, and noisy birds that are equally at home in a town or country setting. This species benefited greatly from the European settlement of North America as forests were turned into farm fields and new feeding and nesting opportunities emerged for the common grackle. Residential areas and farmland are particularly attractive to grackles. Look for long, dark lines of migrating common grackles during the day, especially in fall. Migrating flocks can literally contain thousands of birds and may stretch from horizon to horizon. At feeders grackles relish cracked corn and sunflower seeds most of all. Grackles are also known to take hard, stale pieces of bread and dunk them in a birdbath to soften them.

HOW DO I IDENTIFY IT? Some beginning bird watchers will confuse grackles with starlings, but grackles are noticeably larger birds with much longer tails. In fact, nearly half of the common grackle's 12½-inch length is its tail. The grackle's black plumage is glossy and can show bright purple, bronze, or green highlights, especially on the head. Adult common grackles show a pale yellow eye, which contrasts sharply with their dark head. The powerful bill is long and sharply pointed. In flight, grackles hold their long tails in a "V," much like the keel of a boat. Males and females are very similar in appearance. In the West, you may also see the great-tailed grackle, a much larger species that looks like a common grackle on steroids. Grackles utter a variety of harsh, metallic-sounding tones.

WHERE DO I FIND IT? Common grackles are found in almost every habitat in eastern North America, though in winter the population is more concentrated in the eastern and southern United States. Grackles prefer edge habitat and open areas with scattered trees or shrubs. From late summer to early spring, grackles gather in large roosts with other blackbirds. These roosts can contain as many as half a million birds and are notable both for their noise and their droppings. Spring migrants may reach breeding territories as early as mid-February. Fall migration begins in September and peaks in October.

WHAT CAN I FEED OR DO TO ATTRACT IT? These birds will eat almost anything, so attracting them to a feeder is relatively easy—if you want to do that. Grackles will come to backyards for mixed seed, cracked corn, nuts, and sunflower hearts. During breeding season, grackles eat mostly insects, but they are opportunists and will take nestling birds or eggs, small fish, mice, and frogs. In winter the diet shifts to seeds and grain. The impact of foraging winter flocks on crops has earned the common grackle a reputation as an agricultural pest. Most of the grackle's foraging is done on the ground, where it tosses aside leaves and rubbish to uncover its food. Some people consider these birds backyard pests as well, as the grackles will often dominate the feeders and keep smaller birds from feeding.

NESTING Grackles prefer to nest in dense conifers, close to rich foraging habitat. The large, open cup nest is built by the female from grass, twigs, and mud and is lined with soft grass. She incubates the four to five eggs for about two weeks. The male joins her in feeding the nestlings an all-insect diet until fledging time arrives about 20 days later.

AT A GLANCE	
	—
	✔
	✔
	—
	✔
	✔

Brown-headed Cowbird

The cowbird's habit of laying its eggs in the nests of other, smaller songbirds makes the brown-headed cowbird a nest parasite. Cowbirds learned this behavior over centuries by following roaming herds of bison and cattle. The large mammals stirred up insects, the cowbird's main food. But all the movement made it impossible to stop, build a nest, and wait for the young to grow. So the cowbirds did the most convenient thing—they laid their eggs in any nest they could find along the way. Finding cowbirds is almost never a problem, but limiting their impact on our songbirds can be problematic. Many species are in serious decline because of cowbirds. One way to discourage cowbirds is to stop offering mixed seed and cracked corn during spring when they show up at bird feeders before many migratory songbirds return. If you see a songbird feeding a fledgling that is larger than the songbird, the fledgling is likely a cowbird.

HOW DO I IDENTIFY IT?   The cowbird is a smallish blackbird (7½ inches long). Males have a glossy black body and a dark brown head, while females are a dull gray-brown overall. The short, cone-shaped bill and pointed wings help to distinguish the brown-headed cowbird from larger blackbirds. The cowbird's song is a series of liquid gurgles followed by a high, thin whistle. It's an interesting, unique sound.

WHERE DO I FIND IT?   These birds are found just about everywhere in North America. In Canada and most of the northwestern United States, cowbirds are only present during the summer breeding season. Everywhere else, we have them year-round. Cowbirds are found in a variety of habitats, but they prefer woodland edges, brushy fields, and old pastures, though they are equally at home in city parks and suburban backyards. Forest fragmentation has allowed the cowbird to parasitize the nests of woodland species, such as thrushes and vireos. In winter, cowbirds often join flocks of other blackbirds—red-winged blackbirds, grackles, and European starlings—foraging in fields and grasslands and roosting en masse in large woodlots.

WHAT CAN I FEED OR DO TO ATTRACT IT?   Away from the backyard, cowbirds eat mostly weed and grass seeds, along with insects, especially grasshoppers and beetles. They readily visit feeders for mixed seed and cracked corn. Cowbirds prefer to eat on the ground but will sometimes come to tube feeders. As mentioned, many bird watchers and backyard enthusiasts want to avoid attracting these birds in order to help protect our other songbird species.

NESTING   Male cowbirds court females with a variety of songs, bows, and sky-pointing displays. When she is ready to lay an egg, the female finds a nest that often already contains the eggs of the nest's owner. This "host" nest is most frequently that of a smaller songbird—yellow warblers, song sparrows, red-eyed vireos, and chipping sparrows seem to be frequent victims—and the female cowbird may even remove one of the host's eggs before depositing her own. Hatchling cowbirds are almost always larger than their nest mates and are able to out-compete them for food, enhancing the cowbird's chances of survival. Fortunately, some bird species have evolved to recognize cowbird eggs and will build a new nest on top of the old one or will remove the cowbird egg before it hatches.

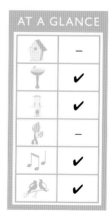

AT A GLANCE	
🏠	–
🍽	✔
🪶	✔
🌾	–
♪♫	✔
🐦	✔

Bullock's Oriole

These brilliant orange-and-black birds brighten up many a western back-yard with their gorgeous plumage and rich, whistling songs. Bullock's orioles spend their summers throughout the western United States but winter in Mexico, where they were first studied in the 1800s. William Swainson, the 19th-century scientist who first described the birds, considered them to be "the most beautiful of the group yet discovered in Mexico." Swainson named the Bullock's oriole after another William, William Bullock, who performed the initial research on this species. This bird and the Baltimore oriole of the East were later lumped together as a single species, the "northern oriole," but were recently separated again as distinct species. The two orioles interbreed frequently where their ranges overlap in the central United States, especially in the Great Plains.

HOW DO I IDENTIFY IT? Bullock's orioles are medium-sized birds (about 8½ inches long) with long tails and long, pointed bills. The adult male Bullock's is hard to miss, his fiery orange-yellow plumage contrasting highly against his jet-black face, back, and wings. While the male Baltimore oriole sports a complete black hood, the Bullock's has black only on the back of the head, around the eye, and on the chin, giving this bird a masked look. Bullock's orioles also tend to be more yellowish overall than their eastern counterparts. Females and young males are plainer, with an overall gray-and-yellow plumage. Young males usually attain the characteristic black throat by October of their first year.

WHERE DO I FIND IT? Look for these birds between spring and fall in open woodlands, parks, suburbs, and backyards throughout the western United States, including much of Texas. They tend to prefer tall, mature trees. Chances are you'll hear a Bullock's oriole before you see it; Bullocks's orioles have a rich, whistled song that's similar to the Baltimore oriole but raspier, with frequent chattering. Males and females both sing. Most of these birds winter in Mexico, though occasionally, some Bullock's orioles show up in the southeastern United States, particularly in Florida, as rare winter visitors.

WHAT CAN I FEED OR DO TO ATTRACT IT? Away from feeders, orioles eat insects (especially caterpillars), spiders, a wide variety of fruits, and nectar. Some of the best ways to lure these birds to your backyard include offering orange and grapefruit halves, grape jelly, or sugar water. Special oriole feeders are available that make it very easy to offer these unique items at your feeding station. You can try planting fruit-producing shrubs, such as serviceberry, and nectar-producing vines, and orioles are also easily attracted with a good birdbath featuring moving water.

NESTING Oriole nests are quite unique. It is usually the female who constructs the hanging, bag-shaped nest near the end of a large branch toward the top of a tall tree. The nest is made of plant fibers, string, and other material. During spring and summer, you can try placing short pieces (2" or less) of loose string around your yard for the birds to use as nesting material. It can be fun to watch the orioles take advantage of your handy supply as they construct a nest in or near your backyard. The female incubates four or five bluish or grayish eggs for about two weeks. Both parents help feed the nestlings until the young birds leave the nest, typically about two weeks after hatching.

AT A GLANCE

🏠	–
🛁	✔
🪶	✔
🌿	✔
🎵	✔
🐦	✔

Purple & Cassin's Finch

The male purple finch is a rich raspberry-red (not purple) color and is often confused with the more common male house finch (which is orange- or brick-red). Purple finches travel in flocks during the non-breeding seasons and may descend on feeding stations for a few hours or several weeks as they roam in search of a winter food source. In some areas, purple finches are in serious decline due to the more aggressive house finch. Another common red-purple finch of the West is the Cassin's finch, which is very similar overall to the closely related purple finch. The purple finch is pictured.

HOW DO I IDENTIFY IT? "Like it was dipped headfirst in raspberry wine" is how many bird watchers describe the color of the male purple finch, and it's an apt description, because the raspberry color completely encircles the bird's upper body. Large-headed with a stout bill, the purple finch is hard to miss, often announcing its arrival with a loud *pik!* call. Their song, which is sung beginning in late winter, is a loud, rich warble delivered from a treetop perch. Females are brown-backed with dark brown and white face patterns and dark cheek patches. Their white breasts are boldly streaked with brown. Cassin's finches are very similar in appearance to purple finches but have thinner, more pointed bills and longer tails. The male Cassin's is generally more pinkish than the purple, and the females are plainer brown, not quite as boldly patterned as female purple finches.

WHERE DO I FIND IT? Purple finches spend the summer throughout the northern boreal forests of Canada and then move into the eastern United States for the winter months. They are year-round residents along the West Coast and throughout the northeastern part of the United States. During the breeding season, you'll find purple finches in a variety of woodland habitats, from cool coniferous woods to deciduous forests, orchards, and edge habitats. Cassin's finches are found year-round throughout much of the western United States, favoring coniferous forests. Both species are easily attracted to your backyard feeders, especially in winter.

WHAT CAN I FEED ON DO TO ATTRACT IT? Purple and Cassin's finches come to feeders for both striped and black-oil sunflower seeds and for thistle seed. Like most other finches, these birds prefer tube feeders. They will also eat suet, peanut bits, and fruit. Away from the feeders, seeds, blossoms, buds, and fruits make up most of their diet, though they also eat insects. Favorite food trees include elms, tulip poplars, maples, dogwoods, sweet gums, sycamores, and ashes. Typical foraging involves a flock of these finches ranging amid upper branches, grabbing and eating young buds. Both species can also be attracted with moving water for drinking and bathing, so think about adding a birdbath.

NESTING In both species, females do most of the nest-building after a pair chooses a site in the outer branches of a large tree, usually a conifer but can sometimes be an aspen or other deciduous tree. She weaves together bark strips, rootlets, and twigs into a cup and lines it with animal hair and fine grass. Three to seven eggs are deposited and incubated by the female for about two weeks. Cassin's finches generally lay only four or five eggs. Both purple and Cassin's finch parents feed their hatchlings until fledging, which typically occurs two weeks after hatching.

AT A GLANCE

🏠	—
🛁	✔
🕯	✔
🌱	✔
🎵	✔
🐦	✔

House Finch

Bird watchers who rely on an eastern field guide that is more than thirty years old may be forgiven for some confusion. This bird won't be in it! The house finch, native to the West, is a well established but recently arrived resident of the eastern United States. When legislation forbidding the trade of wild birds was passed in 1940, a small number of caged house finches were released on Long Island. These birds began to breed and the population exploded almost overnight. Now we have house finches galore across the eastern United States. These aggressive birds have put a lot of pressure on the closely related purple finch, a species that is now in serious decline in the East. Despite the negative connotations associated with these birds, house finches are colorful little birds that produce one of the most musical songs of our common backyard birds. Listen for the male singing persistently throughout the spring and summer from a nearby rooftop, telephone wire, or tall tree.

HOW DO I IDENTIFY IT? People who feed birds are familiar with the house finches that sometimes cover feeders with fluttering, tweeting flocks. It's easy to see why they were kept as cage birds; the male's cheery, rich song, marked by a few harsh notes, tumbles brightly down the scale. Females are streaky, pale brown birds with white undersides; males have a rich pinkish red rump, head, and upper breast. By comparison, male purple finches have an overall "dipped in wine" look, with a reddish suffusion to their back and wings, while female purple finches are much more boldly streaked with brown and white than are female house finches. At first, many bird watchers struggle with keeping house and purple finches apart, but once you become familiar with these birds, the differences become more obvious.

WHERE DO I FIND IT? As its name suggests, the house finch prefers nesting and feeding near homes. It's a thoroughly suburban bird in the East, but in its native West, it is found in undisturbed desert habitats as well. This species appears to be developing migratory behavior in the East, with a general movement toward the South in winter. House finches have also been introduced in Hawaii.

WHAT CAN I FEED OR DO TO ATTRACT IT? For most feeding station proprietors, the question is not how to attract house finches, but how to discourage them. Even attractive birds with pleasant songs wear out their welcome when they descend in dozens, monopolizing feeders. Black oil sunflower seeds are a favorite, closely followed by thistle and mixed seeds. Some people resort to removing perches from tube feeders, thus discouraging house finches, which are poor clingers. Most of the house finch's diet is vegetarian, and it spends a great deal of time feeding on the ground. Weed seeds, buds, and fruits are its mainstays away from feeding stations.

NESTING House finch nests are shallow twig platforms with a finely woven inner cup composed of rootlets, grass, feathers, and string. They are tucked into dense ornamental evergreens, hanging baskets, ledges, ivy-covered walls, and other nooks where there is an overhanging structure. Two to five eggs are incubated by the female, while the male feeds her. Young are fed regurgitated seeds and fledge from 12 to 16 days later.

Pine Siskin

This slender, streaky little finch is often overlooked—mistaken for a female house finch, a winter-plumaged goldfinch, or just "a little brown bird." But a closer look reveals a slender-billed, finely streaked finch adorned with yellow in its wings and tail. Though commonly found throughout the United States each winter, pine siskins are among those northern finch species—along with crossbills, redpolls, and evening grosbeaks—that periodically invade the United States from the far North in large numbers. What happens is the normal food supply (forest seed crops) in the northern forests suffers a dramatic decline and forces the birds to travel widely in search of abundant supplies. If you have a well-stocked feeding station, you may see large flocks of siskins in your backyard during invasion winters. Thistle seed (nyjer) is a favorite of pine siskins.

HOW DO I IDENTIFY IT?   Your first clue to a pine siskin's presence may be its loud, descending *tzeeeew!* call as a flock drops into your backyard trees. Siskins also give a rising *zweeeeet!* sound and sing a jumbled twitter of notes similar to a goldfinch's song. Fine brown streaks cover the pine siskin's body, but as the bird moves, its yellow wing stripes and tail spots flash—a surprise bit of color on this otherwise drab bird.

WHERE DO I FIND IT?   Across the Midwest and the eastern United States the pine siskin is a winter visitor. It nests in the coniferous forests of the far North and throughout the West but makes nearly annual appearances throughout eastern North America. During spring and summer, pine siskins are never far from conifers, alders, and the mixed woodlands in which they breed and forage. In winter, siskins often move southward—sometimes in great numbers—in search of food. They forage in weedy fields, hedgerows, and pine woods and at backyard feeding stations. Listen for the sharp, zippy calls of siskin flocks as they fly over. And be sure to look carefully at your flocks of drab winter goldfinches—a siskin may be accompanying them.

WHAT CAN I FEED OR DO TO ATTRACT IT?   Add a thistle feeder and seed to your backyard offerings and you'll increase your chances of attracting siskins. Look for these tiny seeds wherever you buy wild bird supplies. You can also obtain feeders specifically designed for thistle seed. Siskins are also attracted to sunflower bits. Siskins eat grass and weed seeds, especially wild thistle seeds, plus tree buds, pine seeds, berries, and some insects. Expert clingers, siskins will hang upside-down on a catkin clump, pinecone, or weed stem and pry seeds loose with their finely pointed bills. Pine siskins readily come to birdbaths with moving water.

NESTING   Male siskins begin courting females in late winter, before reaching their breeding grounds, as the winter feeding flocks are dispersing. Siskins are known to nest in loose colonies in conifer or mixed conifer-deciduous forests. The female builds the cup-shaped nest out of weed stems, grasses, bark strips, vines, and rootlets and lines it with soft material like animal fur, feathers, thistledown, or moss. She lays three to five eggs and incubates them for about two weeks, during which time the male may bring her food. Both parents feed the nestlings, which leave the nest about 15 days after hatching.

AT A GLANCE	
🏠	–
🛁	✔
🗼	✔
🌾	✔
♪♩	✔
🐦🐦	✔

Lesser Goldfinch

These are the smallest of our North American goldfinches, though only slightly smaller than the familiar American goldfinch. Lesser goldfinches are common throughout the western United States, showing up in open woodlands, weedy fields, and suburban areas, sometimes in large numbers. They flock to backyard feeding stations, often in the company of American goldfinches, pine siskins, and other small, seed-loving birds. Lesser goldfinches actually come in two color forms; the color of the males' backs varies geographically. Male birds in Texas have dark black backs, while more northern and western birds have lighter, olive-green backs. However, young males of both color forms are green-backed until their second year.

HOW DO I IDENTIFY IT? Overall, these are tiny songbirds (about 4½ inches long) with short tails and large, cone-shaped bills, typical of finches. Males are bright yellow below and either black or olive-green above. Both the black-backed and green-backed males have all-black caps. Look for conspicuous white patches in both the wings and tail when these birds are in flight. Females are paler overall, with yellowish underparts and a grayish green back and wings. White wing bars are usually visible in both sexes when the birds are perched. The males sing a jumbled song of whistles and twitters, similar to the American goldfinch but more hurried and a little less musical. These birds are mockingbird wannabes—listen closely to a singing lesser goldfinch and you may pick out some phrases from other birds' songs.

WHERE DO I FIND IT? Look for lesser goldfinches in open woodlands, weedy fields, brushy areas, and backyards throughout the southern two-thirds of the western United States. The lesser goldfinch's range also extends south into parts of South America. Lesser goldfinches are generally resident throughout most of their range, though birds in the more northern areas will move south in winter. Though usually found in small flocks in weedy fields or backyards, these goldfinches sometimes gather into huge flocks consisting of more than one hundred birds. Such flocks usually include other species, such as American goldfinches. During spring and summer, watch for males singing from the tops of tall trees.

WHAT CAN I FEED OR DO TO ATTRACT IT? Like American goldfinches, lesser goldfinches are easily attracted to bird feeders with black-oil sunflower seeds, sunflower hearts, and thistle (nyjer) seed. Specially made tube-style thistle feeders or thistle socks are the best way to offer the tiny black thistle seeds to your backyard birds. Goldfinches are also attracted to seed-producing weeds, so try providing an ample supply of chicory, thistles, knotweeds, goldenrods, and dandelions in your garden. You can also entice these birds with clean, moving water for drinking and bathing.

NESTING Lesser goldfinches sometimes nest late in the summer, especially in the Southwest. The female builds a compact nest of grass, leaves, plant fibers, and strips of bark in a tree or shrub, usually fairly close to the ground. She lines the nest with plant down, feathers, or animal fur. She lays four or five pale blue eggs, which are incubated for about 12 days. The male will usually feed the female while she is incubating the eggs. Both parents feed the nestlings until they fledge, usually about two weeks after hatching. Lesser goldfinches typically nest at least twice, sometimes three times, each year.

AT A GLANCE

🏠	—
🚰	✔
🪹	✔
🌿	✔
🎵	✔
🐦	✔

American Goldfinch

The bright canary-yellow and black plumage of the breeding male American goldfinch has earned this species the nickname "wild canary." These birds are familiar visitors to bird feeders at all seasons, especially in winter, though they may go unnoticed when dressed in their drab winter garb. The goldfinch's undulating flight is accompanied by a twittering call of perchickoree *or* potato chip! *Goldfinches love to drink and bathe in shallow birdbaths and are especially attracted to moving water.*

HOW DO I IDENTIFY IT?   American goldfinches appear very different in summer and winter. The male's brilliant yellow body and black cap in summer give way to a drab, olive-brown plumage in winter. Female goldfinches, though never bright yellow, also lose most of their color. Both sexes retain their black wings and tail year-round. The sweet, high-pitched, warbling song of the male is often given in early spring, just as these small (5-inch-long) birds are beginning to show their first bright yellow feathers.

WHERE DO I FIND IT? The twittering calls of goldfinches will alert you to the presence of these energetic songbirds. Weedy fields, brushy woodland edges, and open habitats with scattered shrubs are the American goldfinch's normal habitats. In the breeding season, they prefer weedy fields with thistles and other seed-producing plants. In winter, goldfinches roam in noisy flocks, seeking food in fields, in gardens, and at backyard feeding stations. These birds are common throughout the United States and southern Canada.

WHAT CAN I FEED OR DO TO ATTRACT IT? The secret to attracting goldfinches to your yard is thistle (nyjer) seed. Look for these tiny seeds wherever you buy wild bird supplies. You can also obtain feeders specifically designed for thistle seed. Hang a few thistle feeders in your backyard and you will likely have goldfinches year-round. These birds also visit for sunflower seeds and peanut bits. Goldfinches are seed-eaters in all seasons, and away from the feeders they consume a huge variety of weed, grass, and plant seeds as well as tree buds. They are attracted to many backyard plants and weeds, including thistles (of course), goldenrods, and dandelions. Goldfinches are agile birds, able to exploit seed sources that other finches cannot by hanging upside-down from seedheads, plant stalks, and bird feeders.

NESTING Goldfinches' nesting season begins late, an adaptation to ensure that nesting occurs when there is the greatest natural abundance of seeds, as well as the soft thistledown that goldfinches use to line their nests. Late June is the earliest nesting time, but peak nesting season is late July, and some nesting occurs as late as September. The site is in a shaded spot in a sapling or shrub and is selected by the pair. The female builds the open cup nest from twigs (attached with spider web), rootlets, and plant stems, and she lines it with soft thistledown or a similarly soft material. Four to six eggs are incubated by the female for about two weeks, with the male bringing food to her on the nest. Both parents tend the nestlings for 12 to 17 days before they fledge. Goldfinches do not fall victim to brown-headed cowbirds, as young cowbirds are unable to survive the all-seed diet fed to nestling goldfinches.

AT A GLANCE

🏠	–
🛁	✔
💡	✔
🌹	✔
🎵	✔
🐦	✔

Evening Grosbeak

Like a supersized goldfinch, the evening grosbeak is a chunky bird that roams around in noisy flocks, seeking its favorite foods: tree seeds and buds, fruits, nuts, and sunflower seeds at bird feeders. A fairly common nesting bird in the far North and western mountain conifer forests, flocks of evening grosbeaks regularly move southward in winter and this is when backyard bird watchers suddenly find this stunning yellow, black, and white bird on their platform feeder, vacuuming up vast quantities of sunflower seed.

HOW DO I IDENTIFY IT?   This large member of the finch family has a huge, pale, seed-crushing bill. At 8 inches, it towers over the goldfinches, house finches, and pine siskins at the feeder. Males are golden mustard-yellow on their body with a dark head and crown and a bright golden eyebrow atop the eyes and bill. Huge white patches stand out on the black wings and these colors flash when a grosbeak is in flight. The female is dull brownish gray overall with some yellow shading on the body and often showing a collar of yellow. Her black wings also have white on them, but not as cleanly marked as on the male. The evening grosbeak's song is a short, hoarse warble, but the sound most commonly heard is their call note: a loud, ringing *clear! clear!*

WHERE DO I FIND IT?   During the spring and summer breeding sea-sons, look for evening grosbeaks in coniferous forests at higher elevations in the West and from the northernmost portions of the Great Lakes states and New England north to the northern forests. In fall and winter, look and listen for flocks of evening grosbeaks foraging in seed- and fruit-producing trees like maples, box elders, ash, and locust trees and at feeding stations. Flocks of evening grosbeaks are almost always calling noisily, so you are likely to hear them before you see them. Flocks often stop to rest in the tops of tall trees, where their chunky size makes them easy to see.

WHAT CAN I FEED OR DO TO ATTRACT IT?   Planting trees and shrubs that produce seeds, fruits, and berries is a great way to entice evening grosbeaks. Species include box elder, maple, ash, cherry, elm, locust, sweet gum, crabapple, poplar, conifers, and almost any deciduous tree that produces large buds. A nice large platform feeder well stocked with gray-striped and black-oil sunflower seed is another powerful draw. Many feeder birds cannot crack open the striped sunflower seeds, but for a grosbeak, these tough-hulled seeds are an easy-open meal. A large, stable birdbath with moving water can also lure gros-beaks. Crushed bits of eggshell or very fine gravel will help them crush and digest seeds in their gizzards.

NESTING   If you live in the breeding range of the evening grosbeak, you may have a chance to see a male courting a female in early spring. He raises his head and tail, lets his wings droop, and sways back and forth, shaking slightly. If this impresses her, she will begin building the nest in a conifer, often very high up. The nest is made of twigs and lined with softer materials, such as grasses and pine nee-dles. Three to five eggs are laid and incubated by the female for two weeks, during which time the male often feeds her. The nestlings are fed by both parents and fledge about two weeks later.

AT A GLANCE	
🏠	—
🛁	✔
🏮	✔
🌿	✔
🎵	✔
🐦	✔

House Sparrow

This is that common little brown bird that you see on city sidewalks, around traffic lights, in shopping mall parking lots, and sometimes inside the shopping mall itself. They're everywhere. Given the abundance of house sparrows today, you might be surprised to learn that less than two hundred years ago there were no house sparrows in North America at all. The birds were introduced here from England in the 1850s to help control wireworms. The house sparrow population spread from a few birds in New York to the entire North American continent in just fifty years. It is one of the world's most successful and widespread species.

HOW DO I IDENTIFY IT? The chunky little house sparrow is known for its constant *cha-deep, cha-deep* calls and for the male's black bib in breeding plumage. Breeding males have a black bill and a contrasting black, gray, and brown head and face pattern. Winter males are a muted version of the breeding plumage. Females are drab gray-brown overall and lack the bib. House sparrows are constantly chirping and are aggressive competitors at feeders and nest sites.

WHERE DO I FIND IT? House sparrows are year-round residents. It's easier to describe where you *won't* find house sparrows because they are practically ubiquitous. Pristine natural habitats—forest, grassland, or desert—that lack human development will also lack house sparrows. Historically, the house sparrow associated with horses (and the seeds and insects in their droppings) and other livestock. Today, house sparrows are found in the most urban of habitats, living on food scraps and nesting in building crevices—though they're still commonly found in horse barns, farmyards, and feedlots.

WHAT CAN I FEED OR DO TO ATTRACT IT? House sparrows are feeding station regulars, especially in towns and cities. Seeds and grains will be on the house sparrow's normal menu throughout the year. In spring and summer, they take advantage of bountiful insect populations. At any time, house sparrows are quick to take food at bird feeders or scraps of food offered directly or indirectly by humans in parks, picnic areas, fast food restaurants, and strip malls. Cracked corn, sunflower seeds, peanut bits, and bread products are favorite foods. Truth be told, if you're one of the few people in America who does not have house sparrows in the backyard, you might want to consider yourself lucky and try to keep it that way. These birds are very aggressive and tend to dominate any backyard feeding station, driving away your other songbirds.

NESTING Males choose a cavity and sing by it to attract the female. Both build the messy nest of grass, weed stems, feathers, paper, and string. The female lays between three and six eggs, which are incubated by both parents for 10 or more days. The parents share feeding duties until the nestlings are ready to fledge at about two weeks. House sparrows often steal nest boxes from bluebirds, swallows, and purple martins (forcing many nest box landlords to use controls and special housing to discourage house sparrows), and they sometimes even kill nest box competitors. To discourage house sparrows from dominating nest boxes, use boxes with interiors less than 5 inches deep, remove their nesting material regularly, and place nest boxes far from buildings and thick shrubbery.

AT A GLANCE	
🏠	✔
🛁	✔
🗼	✔
🌱	✔
♪♩	✔
🐦	✔

Beyond the Backyard
Birding Hotspots
for the West

Lower Rio Grande Valley National Wildlife Refuge
(spring and fall)
3325 Green Jay Road
Alamo, TX 78516
(956) 784-7500
www.fws.gov/refuge/Lower_Rio_Grande_Valley

This is one of the premier birding locales in the nation. At the southernmost tip of Texas, where the Rio Grande meets the Gulf of Mexico, is this refuge, which hosts hundreds of spectacular bird species. The Lower Rio Grande Valley offers bird watchers the opportunity to see many species not found elsewhere in North America. Some of the avian highlights include plain chachalaca, green jay, great kiskadee, red-billed pigeon, Altamira oriole, and ringed kingfisher. Spring and fall are the best times to visit the Lower Rio Grande Valley, when thousands of neotropical migrants pass through this area. These migrants include numerous warblers, vireos, flycatchers, orioles, and tanagers. Plant species number 1,200, there are 300 butterfly species, and more than 520 bird species have been documented within the Valley. The refuge itself encompasses a large area along the Rio Grande. Helpful maps and other info are available online.

Big Bend National Park
(year-round)
P.O. Box 129
Big Bend National Park, TX 79834
(432) 477-2251
www.nps.gov/bibe/index.htm

Big Bend National Park is a paradise for any outdoors enthusiast. 300,000 people visit Big Bend each year for camping, hiking, backpacking, and, of course, birding. Located in southwest Texas along the Mexican border, this park features beautiful desert scenery, rich history and culture, and birds. There are lots of incredible species. Among the avian highlights are golden eagle, zone-tailed hawk, band-tailed pigeon, magnificent and blue-throated hummingbirds, elf owl, Colima warbler, scaled quail, black-tailed gnatcatcher, Scott's oriole, blue grosbeak, black-throated sparrow, and painted bunting. Black bears and mountain lions roam the area. Several highways lead to Big Bend, though the park is located a considerable distance from any towns or cities. Be sure to make adequate preparations before visiting. More information, including checklists of birds commonly seen in various spots within the park, can be found online.

Stillwater National Wildlife Refuge Complex

(spring and fall)
1020 New River Parkway #305
Fallon, NV 89406
(775) 428-6452
www.fws.gov/stillwater

This wetland system in western Nevada is a premier birding hotspot. The Stillwater Complex consists of three refuges located within an 80-mile radius of Reno. This is a great place to catch both spring and fall migration. Numerous waterfowl and shorebirds pass through these wetlands, including black-necked stilts, long-billed dowitchers, and American avocets. Check the website for directions to specific sites, info on area events, and to download a checklist of birds commonly seen in the area.

Sonny Bono Salton Sea National Wildlife Refuge

(winter and spring)
P.O. Box 120
Calipatria, CA 92233
(740) 348-5278
www.fws.gov/saltonsea

This refuge consists of two separate managed units, 18 miles apart. Together these units comprise about 2,000 acres of agricultural fields and wetland habitats in southern California. Hundreds of bird species migrate through and winter here, including cinnamon teal, white-faced ibis, white-tailed kite, black-necked stilt, long-billed curlew, marbled godwit, willet, and American avocet. Cattle, great, and snowy egrets are abundant year-round. A visitor center is located at the junction of Sinclair and Gentry Roads near Calipatria.

Alamosa/Monte Vista/Baca National Wildlife Refuge Complex

(winter and spring)
8249 Emperious Road
Alamosa, CO 81101
(719) 589-4021
www.fws.gov/alamosa

These three refuges represent thousands of acres of wetland habitat in the San Luis Valley of south-central Colorado. The avian highlight here is the sandhill crane: more than 25,000 of these birds migrate through the valley each year. Peak migration for the cranes is usually mid-October and then again in mid-March. Numerous waterfowl species also migrate through, including northern pintails, green-winged teals, and ruddy ducks. Winter in the San Luis Valley means raptors. Watch for bald eagles, northern harriers, rough-legged hawks, and short-eared owls. Other wildlife you may see here includes elk, coyotes, and porcupines. Go online to download maps and bird checklists for each of these refuges.

Bosque del Apache National Wildlife Refuge

(fall and winter)
P.O. Box 280
San Antonio, NM 87832
(575) 835-1828
www.fws.gov/southwest/refuges/newmex/bosque

This refuge represents one of the best birding areas of the West, comprising more than 57,000 acres along the Rio Grande near Socorro, New Mexico. The majority of Bosque del Apache is moist bottomlands and also includes extensive wetlands, farmlands, and riparian forests. The refuge features a visitor center and a 15-mile auto tour loop, which offers spectacular birding opportunities from your vehicle year-round. Best birds include sandhill crane, white-faced ibis, black-crowned night heron, neotropic cormorant, bald eagle, northern harrier, snow and Ross's geese, northern shoveler, and yellow-headed blackbird. The refuge is situated about 8 miles south of San Antonio and 16 miles south of Socorro.

San Pedro Riparian National Conservation Area

(year-round)
1763 Paseo San Luis
Sierra Vista, AZ 85635
(520) 439-6400
www.blm.gov/az/st/en/prog/blm_special_areas/ncarea/sprnca.html

Southeastern Arizona offers some of the best birding on the planet. This region is home to numerous species that are not found anywhere else in the world—in other words, a birder's paradise. Specialties include sulphur-bellied flycatcher, rose-throated becard, Cassin's and Botteri's sparrows, Gambel's quail, greater roadrunner, pyrrhuloxia, canyon towhee, verdin, pygmy nuthatch, greater pewee, hepatic tanager, yellow-eyed junco, and several warblers including Grace's, red-faced, and olive. If you like hummingbirds, you'll hit the jackpot in this part of the world. Arizona hosts 18 species of hummingbirds, including broad-billed, magnificent, Anna's, black-chinned, and broad-tailed. There are dozens of great birding sites within this region; some key places include San Pedro Riparian NCA, Catalina State Park, Tohono Chul Park, Sabino Canyon, Saguaro National Park, Cave Creek Canyon, and Florida Wash. The Tucson Audubon Society (www.tucsonaudubon.org) offers helpful information for birders traveling to southeastern Arizona.

Grays Harbor National Wildlife Refuge

(spring)
100 Brown Farm Road
Olympia, WA 98516
(360) 753-9467
www.fws.gov/graysharbor

Established in 1990 for the protection of important shorebird habitat, these 1,500 acres of intertidal mudflats, salt marsh, and uplands host hundreds of thousands of migrating shorebirds each year. In fact, at Grays Harbor in April and May, birders can witness one of the largest concentrations of shorebirds on the West Coast. Species include western and least sandpipers, long-billed and short-billed dowitchers, semipalmated plovers, black-bellied plovers, and dunlin. The refuge features a trail that allows visitors ample opportunity to view the birds as they peck and probe in the mudflats, fueling up before continuing on to their northern breeding grounds. Many of these birds end up logging over 15,000 miles on their round trips between wintering grounds in South America and their Arctic breeding grounds. Though spring at Grays Harbor offers the best opportunity to see these birds, some shorebirds do come back through in fall in smaller numbers. Some species even spend the winter here, including black-bellied plover and dunlin.

Yellowstone National Park

(year-round)
P.O. Box 168
Yellowstone National Park, WY 82190
(307) 344-7381
www.nps.gov/yell/index.htm

Yellowstone is a popular destination for many outdoor enthusiasts, including bird watchers. The variety of habitats (sagebrush-grasslands, alpine meadows, and whitebark pine forests) means a nice diversity of bird species. Highlights include gray partridge, ruffed grouse, eared grebe, Swainson's hawk, golden eagle, sandhill crane, long-billed curlew, Williamson's and red-naped sapsuckers, gray and Steller's jays, Clark's nutcracker, sage thrasher, MacGillivray's warbler, western tanager, savannah sparrow, and lazuli bunting. A complete checklist with seasonal information is available online. Other wildlife includes bison, elk, moose, mule deer, bighorn sheep, mountain goat, pronghorn, black and grizzly bears, and gray wolf. The park features trails for hiking and bicycling and designated sites for backcountry camping.

Sacramento National Wildlife Refuge Complex

(spring)
752 County Road 99W
Willows, CA 95988
(530) 934-2801
www.fws.gov/sacramentovalleyrefuges

Five national wildlife refuges and three wildlife management areas make up this complex totaling more than 35,000 acres of wetlands and uplands in the Sacramento Valley of California. Located approximately 90 miles north of Sacramento, this area offers incredible year-round birding, though winter tends to be especially good here. Nearly half of the Pacific Flyway's waterfowl population winters in the Sacramento Valley. In November and December, you can expect to see millions of waterfowl, including northern pintails, ring-necked and ruddy ducks, American wigeons, and greater white-fronted, snow, and Ross's geese. Spring brings shorebirds, including black-necked stilts and American avocets. Various herons, egrets, and other waders are plentiful during summer. Specific directions to each of the eight sites can be found online, along with maps and other helpful info should you decide to check out this incredible ecosystem in central California.

Birds I've Spotted

Species/Description: _____

Date/Time of Day: _____

Location (at a feeder? birdhouse?):_____

Special Notes: _____

Species/Description: _____

Date/Time of Day: _____

Location (at a feeder? birdhouse?):_____

Special Notes: _____

Species/Description: _____

Date/Time of Day: _____

Location (at a feeder? birdhouse?):_____

Special Notes: _____

Species/Description: _____

Date/Time of Day: _____

Location (at a feeder? birdhouse?):_____

Special Notes: _____

Species/Description: _____

Date/Time of Day: _____

Location (at a feeder? birdhouse?):_____

Special Notes: _____

Species/Description: _____

Date/Time of Day: _____

Location (at a feeder? birdhouse?):_____

Special Notes: _____

Species/Description: _____

Date/Time of Day: _____

Location (at a feeder? birdhouse?):_____

Special Notes: _____

Species/Description: _____

Date/Time of Day: _____

Location (at a feeder? birdhouse?):_____

Special Notes: _____

Species/Description: _____

Date/Time of Day: _____

Location (at a feeder? birdhouse?):_____

Special Notes: _____

Species/Description: _____

Date/Time of Day: _____

Location (at a feeder? birdhouse?):_____

Special Notes: _____

Species/Description: _____

Date/Time of Day: _____

Location (at a feeder? birdhouse?):_____

Special Notes: _____

Species/Description: _____

Date/Time of Day: _____

Location (at a feeder? birdhouse?):_____

Special Notes: _____

Resources

ORGANIZATIONS

American Bird Conservancy
P.O. Box 249
4249 Loudoun Avenue
The Plains, VA 20198-2237
www.abcbirds.org

American Birding Association
P.O. Box 6599
Colorado Springs, CO 80934-6599
800-850-2473
www.americanbirding.org

Cornell Laboratory of Ornithology
159 Sapsucker Woods Road
Ithaca, NY 14850
800-843-2473
www.birds.cornell.edu

National Audubon Society
225 Varick Street
New York, NY 10014
www.audubon.org/bird/at_home/
HealthyYard_BirdHabitat.html

National Wildlife Federation
Backyard Habitat Program
11100 Wildlife Center Drive
Reston, VA 20190
www.nwf.org/Get-Outside/Outdoor-
Activities/Garden-for-Wildlife.aspx

**The National Wildlife
Rehabilitators Association**
2625 Clearwater Road, Suite 110
St. Cloud, MN 56301
www.nwrawildlife.org/content/
finding-rehabilitator

The Nature Conservancy
4245 North Fairfax Drive #100
Arlington, VA 22203
www.nature.org

North American Bluebird Society
P.O. Box 7844
Bloomington, IN 47407
www.nabluebirdsociety.org

North American Native Plant Society
P.O. Box 84, Station D
Etobicoke, ON M9A 4X1
Canada
www.nanps.org

**Purple Martin
Conservation Association**
301 Peninsula Drive, Suite 6
Erie, PA 16505
www.purplemartin.org

The Purple Martin Society
www.purplemartins.com

PERIODICALS FOR BIRD WATCHERS

Bird Watcher's Digest
P.O. Box 110
Marietta, OH 45750
800-879-2473
www.birdwatchersdigest.com

Watching Backyard Birds Newsletter
P.O. Box 110
Marietta, OH 45750
800-879-2473
www.watchingbackyardbirds.com

Living Bird
Cornell Laboratory of Ornithology
159 Sapsucker Woods Road
Ithaca, NY 14850
800-843-2473
www.birds.cornell.edu

Index

Meet Bill Thompson III

Bill Thompson III has been a bird watcher for more than forty years—much of it in his own backyard. From an early age he knew his life would be intertwined with birds and bird watching; in fact, his grandmother claimed his first word as a baby was "junco." The bird that got him started as a bird watcher was a lone snowy owl that visited his family's Iowa yard when Bill was just seven years old. From that magic moment, Bill has never stopped watching birds for long.

Bill is the editor and co-publisher of *Bird Watcher's Digest,* a magazine started by his family in 1978 in Marietta, Ohio. He is the author of numerous books on birds and nature, including the award-winning *Young Birder's Guide to Birds of North America.* In great demand as a speaker, birding guide, and performer, Bill has watched birds in forty-nine states and more than thirty countries. He is currently vice president and a founding board member of the Ohio Ornithological Society.

Bill lives with his wife, author/artist Julie Zickefoose, and their two children on 80 acres of wooded farmland in Whipple, Ohio. To date, Bill and family have seen and identified 186 bird species on their farm, many of which were attracted to the bird-friendly habitat that Bill and Julie have created there. When he's not birding or traveling in search of birds, Bill enjoys recording and performing with his country rock band the Rain Crows.

You can catch up with Bill via these birdy channels:
Bird Watcher's Digest: www.birdwatchersdigest.com
Bill of the Birds blog: www.billofthebirds.blogspot.com
Twitter: @billofthebirds, @bwdmag
Facebook: Bird Watcher's Digest